GOLFER'S PALETTE

GOLFER'S PALETTE

PREPARING FOR PEAK PERFORMANCE

DR. JOHN EDWIN DEVORE

To order additional copies of this book, contact:
Xlibris
1-888-795-4274
www.Xlibris.com
Orders@Xlibris.com
685690

CONTENTS

To Mom and Dad, my life's caddies and early golf partners. Mom started to smile from heaven on May 16, 1955; and she laughed joyously on August 21, 1955, when I beat Dad the first time. Dad loved his golf and joined Mom on May 15, 1993. His mischievous smile shines every day.

The most difficult subjects can be explained to the most slow-witted man if he has not formed any idea of them already; but the simplest thing cannot be made clear to the most intelligent man if he is firmly persuaded that he knows already, without a shadow of doubt, what is laid before him.

—Leo Tolstoy, 1897

PREFACE

Gowf is a mighty teacher never deviating from its sacred roots, always ready to lead us on ... And I say to ye all, good friends, that as ye grow in gowf, ye come to see things ye learn in every other place ... Ye'll come away from the links with a new hold on life, that is certain if ye play the game with all your heart.
—Michael Murphy

Golf is a marvelous sport and a treasure chest of great stories, rich traditions, nice legends, cherished heroes, and a stellar global history. Complement this inviting perspective with mystical offerings, the prospect of tickled fantasies, and inspired dreams, coupled with a plethora of life's pristine lessons, and a student of playing a ball with a club will quickly recognize that the journey of golf is the destination. However, as the culture of golfers will attest, golf is a sport that is, without question, an open field of friendly strife where peace can prevail—or where mental and emotional chaos has the potential to emerge before every shot, on every shot, and between every shot. On any given day, as my sixty-seven years of golf has proven, the golfer is no less than two shanks, two slices, or two duck hooks from insanity. Fortunately, there are tickets for release from this self-manufactured asylum.

Playing a ball with a club from the teeing ground into the hole by a stroke, or the fewest successive strokes, in accordance with proper etiquette, the current United States Golf Association (USGA) Rules of Golf, ball flight laws, and integrity, has attracted and continues to attract millions of golfers who invest their time and money in enjoying, playing, and learning the game. Our addiction to knowing and the analytical prowess of the mind have generated overwhelming volumes of golf process materials for all levels of golfers and golf professionals. This book is intended to supplement the current golf literature and the high-quality instruction provided by golf professionals.

Drawn from personal golf experiences, a sampling of golf literature, and notes and papers from academic work, *Golfer's Palette* is a simple guide that can support the golfer who has clear golf goals and desires. Because of my preference for coaching, as opposed to teaching, this book needs to be used by those who are inspired to improve personally selected parts of their game. Personal experience speaks loudly that performing on the course, enjoying the game, and learning about the game requires an inquiring spirit, creativity, and a willingness to fail, experiment, and prepare.

Because of my own inquiring spirit, complemented by an interest in research and academics, you will quickly notice that this book contains quotes and footnotes from the works of many professionals. Drawing on this wealth of golf knowledge has been educational and fun. My hope is that, as an interested reader, you will reap benefits from our perspectives.

Golfer's Palette's Introduction provides a glimpse into my background and golfing philosophy. Chapter 1, "The Game and Player," includes a brief look at the game, the culture of golfers, and my personal reflections about golfers. Chapter 2, "Learning and Practice," sets the stage for Chapter 3, "Body-Mind Mastery Skills," an invitation to tame your mind and prepare your body for optimum performance. Chapter 4, "Technical Skills," is a synopsis of the body and club mechanics necessary for consistent play. Chapter 5, "Putting It All Together," facilitates moving from goals and desires to forging your will and playing better golf. A detailed synopsis of my background, experiences, and contact information can be found inside the back cover.

As a reader and golfer, you will soon recognize that the central message of this book is that good golf is playing and practicing a synchronized inner and outer game and that this sport requires absolute trust in your subconscious to create every shot by removing all except the golfer, a club, a ball, a target, and a course. Quite simply, this chosen sport of ours is nothing more than clearing space for the artist within to sculpt a memorable shot.

As Bob Rotella says, "… researchers have discovered that the body of a trained athlete has highly developed 'neural networks' that can subconsciously control the body's movements during execution of a complex athletic skill-like … pitching a golf ball off closely mowed grass, over a bunker, and onto a green so that it stops by the hole."[1]

---

[1] Rotella, 61.

ACKNOWLEDGMENTS

Many teachers, coaches, leaders, and friends have influenced my life and have shown me the way to be awake, have peace of mind, embrace a compassionate response, and behave with honesty, integrity, and morality. Without them, this book would not have been transformed from vision to reality.

A most profound witness has been my wife, Cindy, who is my life and golf partner, coach, and teacher. Every day I am grateful for her patience, wisdom, and love. The kids—Doug, Debbie, and Chris—have offered priceless feedback, counsel, and guidance; and the six grandkids—Kelsie, T. J., Josh, Jasmine, Calista, and Haley—are lights for my continued journey. Family is forever!

A particular note of thanks goes to my son, Doug. He wanted to learn to play golf in the summer of 2004. The first lesson with him at Indian Tree Golf Course, Arvada, Colorado, led to my wife, Cindy, and me taking lessons for six weeks from Tom Thorne at Indian Tree. This was followed with five years of instruction at GOLFTec with Bill Kipp, Patrick Nuber, Chad Wise, Justin Morris, Tony Brooks, and Gabe Hatcher, and fifteen months at The Golf Academy of America–Phoenix with Doug. We graduated in April 2011, and our experiences with weekly tournament golf and instructors Ed Ekis, Ralph Hawley, John Gunby, Tim Wilkins, Dave Hockett, Pete Huber, Jay Friedman, Tim Eberlein, and Gary Balliet are alive in our game today.

My memorable schoolteachers—Ms. Seig, Ms. Schlegel, Olan Smith, Rex Burke, and Mr. Falon—were great enablers. And my spiritual leaders—Father Maumeister, Ringu Tulku Rinpoche, Rabbi Schachter, Brother Micah, Judith Simmer-Brown, Ginger Brooks, and Father Tom Nelson—inspired me by modeling the way as persons, in relationships and when helping me. Bill Coors, General Charles B. Smith, and Bob Morin motivated me with their leadership talents and skills, and Al Goldberg, Alton Barbour, Frank Dance, Trish Jones, and Ron Gist supported my academic pursuits at the University of Denver.

A final thanks to the numerous authors who have contributed priceless additions to my life by choosing to share their wisdom through research and the printed word.

INTRODUCTION

In April 1970, having just completed eight years of military service, including two years of combat during the Vietnam War, I needed to resettle and find a civilian job in either Florida or Colorado. Colorado evolved as an acceptable choice because it was home of my soon-to-be ex-wife and our daughter, Christine.

After two civilian job starts in Denver, a third job with the Adolph Coors Company proved to be a good match for the next twenty-one years. During the first six months there, the boss advised that learning to manage my perfectionist personality type would be a good idea. Fortunately, I listened and immediately launched into what has been a journey of forty-plus years of learning, practicing, and experiencing self-awareness.

Subsequent to my retirement from Coors in 1993, there were again three jobs, a couple of log homes built with my son, Doug, and a commitment to three bowling leagues and forty to fifty games of practice per week. When my average peaked at 208, the self-imposed tension to get it right was still lingering. Burned out from the stress of bowling, I began to search for ways to discover a bridge between my body and my mind. Preliminary research showed that sitting meditation, coupled with noticing and feeling the sensations of breathing, might be the answer.

In pursuit of the link between my mind and body, I chose to study the five wisdom traditions and meditation in the contemplative environment of Naropa University for three years. A highlight of this fascinating experience was a study-abroad program in Sikkim, India. Connected breath, concentration, and meditation became close allies during those years of practice and study, and they remain my friends and close associates, along with bowling, billiards, yoga, and golf.

Two reasonable questions emerge: How could golf, connected breath, concentration, and meditation possibly be connected? Can golf offer friendly grounds on which to practice contemplation, to uncover the fruits of authentic inner power, and to marry interests in philosophy and in sport?

In April 2011, Doug and I graduated from The Golf Academy of America–Phoenix. In 2013, advanced teaching at The Golf Academy of America found this student playing, studying, and coaching golf. I had played golf for six-plus decades, and these studies inspired a deeper interest in the evolving process of learning about golf, coupled with a beginning awareness of, understanding of, and commitment to creating an intimate relationship between my body-mind and the club, ball, target, and course on every shot.

The quality of on-the-course experiences, practice, and learning have been re-energized by my passion for body-mind mastery and for modeling the way as a *person* and in *relationships,* and when *skillfully enabling* others to perform optimally, to touch authentic joy, and to learn and grow in life and in golf.

- *Person*: The essence of our behavior, appearance, and life circumstances are fundamental to gaining and building influence with others. The spiritual masters have said that silence and solitude, coupled with a journey driven by ethics, values, and 100 percent responsibility, can nurture a calm, peaceful state of mind and a purpose-driven life with connections built on a foundation of compassion.

- *Relationships*: We all need witnesses to our lives, and we are, indeed, witnesses to the lives of others. Witnesses are our best teachers, and they mirror our judgments and reflections of the world. In high-quality relationships, our gifts are to each other. And as personalities unfold, we learn to skillfully enable each other to be the best we can be in both life and golf. A high-quality relationship is warm, comfortable, compassionate, open, and egoless.

- *Skillful enabling*: Each golfer is unique, which requires a finely tuned connection between the student and facilitator if performance, enjoyment, and learning are to be optimized for the student. The enabler must want to be with the student *for the student*; and a reasonable goal for the student-coach partnership is for the student to become his or her best coach. Prior to each coaching session, the player and facilitator have a dialogue to fine-tune each session to match the goals and expectations of the student. A menu of development skills can be used to facilitate dialogue and to ensure progressive enjoyment and learning.

Menu of Development Skills

Playing winning golf implies focusing on saving putts, hitting fairways, hitting greens in regulation, and consistently making ups and downs; celebrating and being grateful for the successes, friendships, and the thrills of the walk; and embracing and learning from all opportunities as they are offered. As our games progress, a mutual challenge is to carefully select from a simple list of skills that enable us to transcend to the level of the game for which we are ready.

- *The player*: The player has been and must remain the most important ingredient in this sport, with its exceptionally rich history. A good coach must know and understand the student, and commit to help the student uncover and realize his or her optimum potential; to allow and inspire this potential to emerge; and to support an effective and efficient learning process for the player to meet his or her goals and expectations.
- *The game*: Become an exemplary student of the game by learning golf's history, the Rules of Golf, etiquette, and pace-of-play.
- *Technical skills*: Become technically proficient through an awareness and an understanding of logistical factors, ball flight laws, swing principles, equipment, and games within the game. A critical element of this process is knowing how each swing *feels*. Experience offers knowledge of how the overall feel of an effective swing can be conducive to replicating that swing time after time.
  1. Develop the technical skills that work for you. Steer clear of the tips, tipsters, and quick fixes.
  2. Golf technical skills and talents are transferrable from one club to other clubs.
  3. A good set-up acronym is GASP: grip, aim, stance, and posture.
  4. The key elements of each shot are body mechanics, club mechanics, ball position, routines, rituals, and swing motion.
  5. The games within the game include putting, short game (chipping, pitching, and bunker shots; shots thirty yards and less to the hole); scoring wedges (thirty to one hundred yards to the hole); and long-power game (long irons, fairway woods, hybrids, and driver).
  6. Being able to sense static and dynamic balance is a prerequisite to learning other technical golf skills.

- *On the course*: This includes warm-up; playing lessons that integrate skills; practicing tension detection and release; becoming aware of and understanding the golf shot cycle; learning to create and practicing the creation of personal space—your own teepee for each shot; becoming a master of putting; and loving the short game.

- *Learning and practice*: We each must uncover how we learn best; and our practice needs to integrate skills and closely replicate play on the field of friendly strife. Awareness is our best teacher, and it is the primary faculty we have for knowing and learning from experience. Awareness of experiential sensations—the language of the muscles that must provide the body mechanics to optimize club to ball contact at impact—is critical. If the golfer wants to change something, a first step is to increase his or her awareness of the way it is: just focus on a specific area or sensation and become more aware of what is there. There are many times when our human system self-corrects. Contemplative learning can also be a powerful asset. This concept involves hearing or reading information; brewing it; and just being with it to move from knowing the information to experiencing the information in our behavior.

- *Body-Mind Mastery*: Accept the 100 percent responsibility challenge and commit to the principle that life happens because of us and not to us. A good night's sleep is always critical for optimum performance. A well-balanced diet can improve energy levels; and regular, targeted physical exercise (cardiovascular, power and endurance, and stretching) can prevent injuries to core muscles, shoulders, wrists, and the lower back. Planned exercise can also help us prepare for optimum performance, boost our attitude and motivation, and ease stress and anxiety. The regulation of breathing, combined with good set-up, concentration, and meditation, can facilitate the release of tension and the flow of a supple body, mind, and emotions to each shot at impact of the club through the ball and to the target.

As performance, enjoyment, and learning progress, body-mind mastery becomes 80 to 90 percent of the game. The challenge is to learn to be present, to watch our thoughts, feelings, and body sensations, and not to nurture the pesky dysfunction of the egoic mind. Learning to notice the breath, to be at peace, to develop the capacity for targeted concentration, and to trust our subconscious to perform can become real assets as we prepare to pull the trigger to move the club through the ball to the target.

1. Learn to sense and release tension in your system. Stress undermines peak performance and is the ruination of more on-the-course and practice swings by both amateurs and professionals than any other cause.

2. Understand and commit to nurture those values and principles that enable a peak performance state to emerge, on and off the course.

3. Uncover a meditation practice that works for you and find a good meditation instructor. As used here, *meditation* covers specific terms denoting techniques and practices designed to concentrate and focus your mind on what you choose, for as long as you choose.

Regardless of the level of commitment to the sport, it is very important to search for a coach who has the motivation to grow and to nourish means that are *simple, accurate,* and *practical.* Each student is an original, and some key principles for coaches to consider are as follows:

- Help the student learn as he or she learns best. As Ed Shoemaker said, "The genius resides in the student, not in the coach. The coach's primary job is to help the student become aware of that genius and remove the barriers that hinder it."[2]
- Do nothing by halves, and remain committed to 100 percent responsibility. Remember, life happens because of us and not to us.
- Maintain balance in your physical body, thinking, feeling, and essence, and remain committed to health, wellness, and well-being.
- Pursue authentic joy as a journey, never forgetting that the destination is the journey.
- Live the virtues of supportiveness, respect for life, sincerity, compassion, courage, genuineness, patience, and humility.
- Embrace the critical importance of human equality. We are all fundamentally the same, are in search of unconditional love, and are on a never-ending quest to attain authentic joy and avoid suffering. As the Dalai Lama reminds us, "Despite all our individual characteristics, no matter what education we may have or what social rank we may have inherited, and irrespective of what we may have achieved in our

---

[2] Shoemaker, 102.

lives, we all seek to find happiness and to avoid suffering during this short life of ours."[3]

As a student of golf, seven key goals to consider are as follows:

- To have a good club fitter.
- To play with golf clubs and golf balls that fit and feel good.
- To learn from a menu of golf skills: putting; short game (pitching, chipping, and sand shots); scoring wedges; and using power clubs— long irons, driver, fairway woods, and hybrids. Learning these skills includes club mechanics, body mechanics, routines, rituals, ball position, and swing motion.
- To learn about the game, study history, etiquette, ball flight laws, Rules of Golf, and pace-of-play.
- To select good golf coaches who are technically qualified and committed to skillfully and efficiently helping you learn the skills and processes of the game. This includes keeping practice carefully targeted at play on the course—that is, practicing golf as you play golf on the course.
- To evolve the process and capacity to create a concentrated, trusting, clear, and quiet state when preparing to pull the trigger for every golf shot on the course and during practice.
- To become aware of, understand, and commit to the concept of awareness in life and golf. A significant challenge is to grasp the unique nature of the concept of awareness: if something needs to change, it will change as we increase our awareness of it.

The golf industry is continuing to groom traditional, institutionalized teachers and managers. It needs new, visionary leaders who can sculpt a future and intentionally influence and coach others to move from current reality toward a future that serves individuals, families, communities, and an evolving human consciousness. As Dana Garmany, chief executive officer of Troon Golf, a premier golf management company, states,

> You can't get a 35 year-old to love golf in the same way you
> get a 60 year-old ... We need to resell the game to the younger
> generation ... People have fewer discretionary hours, a greater focus

---

[3] His Holiness the Dalai Lama, 29.

on family, less interest in exclusivity and less acceptance for rule ...
But two things remain constant: people love the conditioning and
beauty of the golf course, and people like to have fun with friends ...
We have to get people in groups to play golf ... Golf is a difficult
game ... People need friends they can struggle with ... With group
lessons we have a better chance of keeping new players ... golf
teachers need to talk to students and help them incrementally ...
people have less time and do not want to reinvent their swings ...
They want to play with their friends and have fun ... We need fathers
to be able to play with their sons-just hit some balls together ... The
next five years, golf will deal with economic troubles ... after that golf
will deal with demographic troubles ... Golf has avoided a complete
free-fall because of baby boomers. But in 10 years that generation
will have passed its peak for playing golf, and the next generations
are not playing golf like their fathers did.[1]

Add to these challenges the fact that today the number of golf facilities far
exceeds the demands for such facilities. Just a few years ago, 60 percent of golf
in the United States was played at private country clubs. Today, 60 percent is
played at semi-private clubs, where the public has been invited to play to keep
the facilities operating. The time has come for new leadership and vision for
an industry that is a giant engine waiting to be fired, stoked, and given rebirth.

This new vision will evolve as each individual makes one step at a time. As
Eckhart Tolle remarks, "Life is the dancer, and you are the dance."[5] Some ideas
for your next steps are as follows:

- Practice following your breath, focusing on your point of origin,
  deepening your concentration, and allowing your subconscious to
  activate muscles as they have been programmed to act. The conscious
  mind does not speak the language of the subconscious; however,
  developing a clear and quiet state of mind can offer the environment
  for uncorking the spontaneous creativity of your subconscious mind
  for every golf shot.
- Learn to meditate, and use contemplation to develop mindfulness,
  awareness, and a clear and quiet state of mind to inspire creativity in
  every shot.

---

[1] Crittenden, 28–31.
[5] Tolle, 115.

- Become a student, your best coach, and a master of life, golf, and the human system.
- Become intimately aware of and understand the ego; commit to being present and to transcending the ego on and off the course.
- Become aware of, understand, and watch for positive and negative emotions on the course.
- Commit to health, wellness, and well-being. A balanced human system nurtured by meditation, good sleep, exercise, and nutrition can foster the flow of the conscious mind, physical body, and subconscious mind at impact on every shot.
- Be 100 percent responsible and alert for causes. Do not be distracted by effects, tips, and tipsters.
- Have fun, learn, and perform to the best of your ability.

In closing, here are parting thoughts to ponder: Michelangelo frescoed the ceiling of the Sistine Chapel by removing gold stars against a blue background painted by Pier Matteo d'Amelia; and he removed marble from a marble block until *David* appeared. The golfer in a pristine, clear, and quiet state creates each shot by removing all except the supple human system, a club, a ball, a target, and the course. Peak performance golf demands that we spark our artistry and trust our subconscious to unleash fruits on every shot. As a good cowboy friend remarked, "John, this is nothing more than clearing away the horse manure and just hitting a golf ball to a target." And Tim Gallwey offers this: "Few games provide such an ideal arena for confronting the very obstacles that impair one's ability to learn, perform, and enjoy life, whether on or off the course."[6] As good golfers, our mutual challenge is to learn, practice, reflect, and experience the integration of technical and body-mind mastery skills. Quite simply, we just need to accept the opportunity to play synchronized inner and outer games.

---

[6] Gallwey, 8.

CHAPTER 1

The Game and Player

Introduction

Golf is an exemplary example of a sport with charismatic heroes, a fascinating history, bonding traditions, many legends, amazing stories, awesome mystical experiences, and seductive qualities. Add to this splash of magnetism the fact that the course is a classroom that enables the five-sensory to multisensory evolution of the human species and that reveals naked truths about life, we have something quite special.

It is an honor, privilege, and pleasure to be a playing member of the culture of golfers and the institution of golf. Whether they are professional golfers, ardent golfers, weekenders, occasional golfers, or students of the game, it is beginning to seem that almost all golfers have chosen to use the sport of golf as a spiritual practice. As Adam Greene shares with his golf associates in *Golf in the Kingdom*, "Golf is the new yoga of the supermind."[7]

We may not consciously choose the process of the game to be a spiritual practice; it just is. Our efforts might be to seek improvement, to study, to learn, or to rehearse; to test our perseverance or patience; to polish up and sharpen up; or merely to keep trying to become proficient and to uncover the unknown pleasures to be gained from an alluring, often frustrating, sometimes mystical, but always humbling game.

It has taken me more than sixty-seven years to begin to appreciate the creative efforts of Michael Murphy and his mystical masterpieces *Golf in the Kingdom* and *The Kingdom of Shivas Irons*. Moreover, experience has certainly

---

[7] Murphy, 52.

helped to prod my awareness that as golfing proficiency evolves, we must accept the challenge to play both the inner and the outer games. As members of the culture of golfers, we begin to recognize that we are really jugglers who need to manage and integrate many technical and body-mind mastery skills on and off the course.

The offerings of this chapter include a brief history of the game, some thoughts about etiquette and rules of the game, reflections concerning equipment, a discussion of the games within the game, and a peek at those of us who play the game.

The Game

History

No one has been able to precisely establish when and where golf began. These first ancestors may have been Roman soldiers playing *paganica;* perhaps the Chinese during the Ming dynasty; the English during the middle of the fourteenth century; or the French, who played *jeu de mail*, imported from Italy. In any case, the game of golf as we know it today has a rich history.

The first written evidence was found at St. Andrews Links, Fife, Scotland, dated to as early as 1552. Their first golf club was organized in 1754. The golf bug hit America in 1888, as John Reid, the father of American golf, and five of his friends gathered in a cow pasture in Yonkers, New York, to socialize and give golf a try. November 14, 1888, marked the official beginning of golf in America with the founding of St. Andrews Golf Club in Yonkers, New York.[x]

Since its early beginning, the sport of golf has been witness to an evolution of equipment changes; numerous success stories about professional golfers like Bobby Jones, Ben Hogan, Sam Snead, Jack Nicklaus, Annika Sorenstam, Tiger Woods, and Phil Mickelson; an overwhelming number of successful golf teaching professionals, such as David Leadbetter, Joseph Parent, Butch Harmon, Jim McClean, and Todd Sones; and a myriad of golf management and teaching professionals in golf facilities and management companies. The 2005 "Golf Economy Report," conducted by SRI International and commissioned by the leadership of Golf 20/20, indicated that the total economic impact of the golf industry in the United States was $195 billion, including two million jobs and $61 billion in wage income. The most recent international growth of golf is occurring in China and Eastern Europe.

---

[x] Peper, 11–89.

Let's Play Golf

The game of golf is played against the course and oneself; the score may be an indication of how well a golfer has mastered the necessary technical and body-mind mastery skills. Playing a ball with a club from the teeing ground into the hole by a stroke, or fewest successive strokes—in accordance with proper etiquette, the current USGA Rules of Golf, and ball flight laws—can be both a relaxing and a pressure-filled experience.

The strokes require exceptional conceptual and experiential talents and skills. The litany of technical, mental, physical, and emotional talents and skills is extensive and complex. Each golf shot requires that the conscious mind be gainfully occupied, that a physical body swing be triggered with exemplary club mechanics, and that a well-trained, subconscious mind be trusted to orchestrate a technically sound, smooth, fluid swing that delivers the clubface through the ball to a desired target.

Playing consistent, good golf requires that, for each shot, you are present and plan to have an environment where peak performance has the potential to emerge. This is a tough assignment; being in-the-zone demands exceptional *preparation, transition, and action*. The majority of *preparation* happens on the practice tee and away from the golf course, so we develop body-mind mastery skills and solid technical skills. Michael Lardon suggests that the following aptitudes need to be developed for in-the-zone artistry to occur: passion for dreaming, capacity to transform desire into will, balance of conscious control with subconscious control, simplicity coupled with positive thought processes, ability to remain in the present moment, ability to be process-driven, management of thoughts and emotions, pure motivation, self-confidence, ability to perform under pressure, acceptance, and faith that enables conquering fear.[1]

The *transition* part of the sport is warming up our bodies and minds before we march off to the first tee. This topic will be addressed in detail in Chapter 5, "Putting It All Together." However, it is important to say that warming up the human system before play is important if our goal is to do the best we can on every shot.

The *action* is quite simple: during setup, we are able, at will, to draw upon and integrate a palette of tools to enable a clear and quiet state to emerge as we pull the trigger for each shot and trust our subconscious to perform as it has been programmed.

---

[1] Lardon and Leadbetter, *Finding Your Zone*.

Rules and Etiquette

Every player is responsible for knowing the rules and etiquette of golf. Nothing is more frustrating than to play with a golfer who has not taken the time to become familiar with these aspects of the game. To help you become familiar with definitions, etiquette, and rules, strongly consider purchasing these two books: *Golf Rules Illustrated, The Official Publication of the United States Golf Association* and the pocketbook version of *The Rules of Golf, United States Golf Association*. Both of these books are updated every two years and can be purchased at www.usga.org or at most golf equipment stores. Also consider keeping the pocketbook version of *The Rules of Golf* in your golf bag.

Pace-of-Play

Slow play is the single most perplexing problem in the game of golf. A slow player can ruin the day for all players behind him or her. In the interest of all, players have an obligation to play at a reasonable pace. An added variable in the pace-of-play equation is the number-one revenue producer on golf courses: greens fees. Course management has an obligation to its board or management team to fill as many tee times with foursomes as are available. From this perspective, pace-of-play becomes a team effort between golfers and course management.

The United States Golf Association (USGA) has launched five pace-of-play initiatives to promote a more enjoyable and sustainable game. This effort consists of research and education elements as follows:

- analysis of key factors known to influence pace-of-play: course design, course management and setup, player management, and effectiveness of player education programs
- research by the USGA Test Center to produce Pace-of-Play Modeling based on quantifiable data drawn from extensive inputs
- a pace rating system that the Test Center Pace-of-Play Model will use to drive improvements in the USGA Pace Rating System
- on-site assistance at golf courses, including new programs to help golf course managers assess and improve pace-of-play—delivered by the USGA Green Section through its Turf Advisory Service; also the expansion of educational efforts, and onsite visits to evaluate the overall playing quality of a golf course
- player education programs

Pace-of-play guidelines from The Golf Academy of America-Phoenix's Conditions of Competition for GAA Tournaments state,

> The pace-of-play will be constantly monitored. A group is out of position if it has an open hole ahead and it has taken more than an average of 14 minutes per hole (4 hours, 12 minutes for an 18 hole round of golf). A group, which is out of position, may be warned, but a warning is not required. A player is allowed 30 seconds to make a stroke after it is clearly his-her turn to play. Players will be notified of violations, but more than one violation may occur during play of a hole. A second violation will result in a two-stroke penalty. A third violation will result in disqualification.

Sunland Springs Village Golf Club, Mesa, Arizona, offers the following pace-of-play guidelines in its "Rules of Ready Golf."

On the Tee

1. The player who is ready should hit.
2. Shorter hitters should hit first.
3. Tee off as soon as the group ahead is clear.
4. Carry an extra ball in your pocket.

On the Fairway

1. Hit when ready and safe; do not use honor system.
2. Take appropriate clubs to your ball and hit without delay.
3. Have your group watch where each shot goes.
4. Limit search for lost balls to three minutes.
5. Pick up and place ball on green upon reaching double par.

On the Green

1. Place your clubs between green and next tee.
2. Study your putt while others are putting.
3. Continue putting until holed out.
4. Leave the green immediately after holing out and proceed to the next tee. Complete your scorecard after you're off the green.

On Par 3 Greens

- Upon reaching the green, if the group in front of you is waiting to hit on the next tee, stand in a safe area and have the group behind you hit.

Short Cuts

1. Mark your score on the way to the next tee.
2. When driving a cart, drop your partner at his or her ball, then continue to your ball.

Ready Golf Enforcement Policy

1. If you fall more than one shot behind, our staff will issue a warning.
2. If you remain behind, you will be asked to forfeit your tee or skip a hole.
3. If these steps do not solve the problem, you can be asked to leave the course for the benefit of the other golfers.

Remember, slow play affects everyone. Please cooperate for the enjoyment of all.

THANK YOU!

As members of the culture of golfers, each of us can contribute to pace-of-play efforts on the courses we choose to play:

- Be your own best pace-of-play coach by identifying the ways you can pick up the pace-of-play.
- As a general guideline, before going to each green with your putter, it helps pace-of-play when golf cars and golf clubs are parked or placed between the green on which you are putting and the next teeing ground.
- Give "Tee It Forward" a try: play from a set of tees best suited to your driving distance.
- Practice "ready golf" during stroke play: when you are ready to shoot, shoot!
- Serve as an example for those around you.
- Embrace opportunities to play nine holes.

- Give alternate formats a try: match play, Stableford, four-ball, and other formats like Speed Golf, and two-ball-Chapman.
- Play more quickly, play better, and have more fun.
- Go to www.usga.com to learn about USGA publications, programs, and suggestions for further reading concerning pace-of-play.

Equipment

Essential ingredients for good golf are a qualified club fitter and equipment that fits well and feels right. A good set of clubs helps scoring and allows you to hit decent shots. No matter where you are on the golf course, you would like to hit the ball as close to the pin as possible, so you want a set of clubs that will do that with the fewest strokes and as consistently as possible. As you reflect on putting together a "game plan" for equipment, consider the following:

- Enjoyment of the game is enhanced because properly fitted clubs look, feel, perform, and sound good. Spend time experimenting with different golf balls; you may want to consider being fitted for a golf ball that is matched to your club-head speed. Good-fitting golf shoes are a must.
- Performance is enabled with good equipment, because equipment that doesn't fit will not optimize your club and body mechanics. Proper equipment can prevent those dreaded pushed and pulled shots.
- Learning is more fun, efficient, and effective with fitted clubs, because they create key variable in the learning process.
- Do not shop for golf club equipment unless you have your specifications in hand and you know exactly what you intend to purchase. Golf club technology is a moving target, and marketers can reel you in very quickly with new head designs, grips, and shafts that are being mass-produced and hitting the shelves every month. Normally, these manufacturers ship standard specifications with wide manufacturing tolerances. Unfortunately, golf games are not improving; money is being wasted on equipment that does not meet advertised expectations; and, more than likely, the newfangled club does not meet either your expectations or your personal equipment specifications.

Some items to expect from a qualified and reputable club fitter are as follows:

- Determine what the golfer is seeking in a new set of golf clubs; how he or she perceives the game; his or her perceived skills, talents, strengths and limitations; a budget for new equipment; and his or her golf goals and objectives.
- Determine acceptable club head design in relation to the player's ability.
- Establish the proper lengths of clubs, because that is the basis for consistency and accuracy.
- Determine the proper lie for the clubs, because that is a key for accuracy.
- Establish the proper face angle, because that is a critical variable for direction.
- Establish necessary lofts, a variable that is key for trajectory and distance.
- Determine the club shaft specifications: the shaft is the engine for the golf club and is critical for optimum distance and physical comfort for the golfer.
- Determine the optimum grip size, because the grip establishes the relationship between the golfer's hands and the club; a proper fitting grip is absolutely essential because live hands enable the golfer to feel the club head and control the swing.
- Optimize the weight of the golf club for optimum playability.

If you are interested in further exploring the art of club fitting, consider investing in *Total Clubfitting in the 21st Century: A Complete Program for Fitting Golf Equipment* (Hierko Trading Company, 800-367-8912).

Games within the Game

The games within the game are certainly not rocket science. If you are new to the game, learn them in the order listed below. Why? Many of the basic skills we learn at the outset are transferrable as we progress up our learning curve. Work especially hard on good fundamentals, because in the future they will offer dividends on the course and in practice. Some of the early skills are grip; proper aiming; a comfortable stance and good posture that permit sensing static and dynamic balance; ball position; and a fluid swing motion that requires proper body and club mechanics. Here are the games within the game:

- Short game
  -Putting: putts up to six feet and lag putts
  -Chipping and chi-putting: normally up to twenty yards
  -Pitching: normally shots up to thirty yards, with spin and without spin
  -Sand shots: greenside and fairway bunkers
- Scoring wedges: thirty to 110 yards to hole
- Long game: 110 yards and longer to the green
- Body-mind mastery: physical, mental, and emotional skills
- On the course: synchronize the inner and outer games, enjoy the walk, strategize, do your best and uncover how good you are as you learn, perform, and play the game.

Player

As members of the culture of golfers, on every shot each of us needs to learn, practice, and use our unique ability to juggle many, many technical and body-mind mastery skills. Here are a few in the technical arena: ball flight laws, swing principles, clubs and club fitting, club and body mechanics, ball position, and setup and swing motions for a variety of shots. In the body-mind mastery area are the capacity to quiet the mind at will and to remain in the moment for as long as desired; an evolving awareness of the ego and its relation to the mind and emotions; the precision and perfection the game requires; the pressures of friendly competition; the unique pace of the game; and an obsessions with "do this, do that" swing motions for various shots.

The player has been and must remain the most important ingredient in a sport with an exceptionally rich history. As players, it is critical that we become aware of how we learn best, coupled with creative strategies that optimize our abilities to become our best coach. If you choose to enlist the services of a coach, he or she must know, understand, and commit to helping you uncover the potential that is within you; to allow and inspire your inner spirit to emerge; and to support an effective and efficient learning process for you to meet expectations and to transform your goals and desires into action.

CHAPTER 2

Learning and Practice

Introduction

The learning and practicing challenges and opportunities of golf are many! As Tim Gallwey writes in *The Inner Game of Golf,*

> Golf has an uncanny way of endearing itself to us while at the same time evoking every weakness of mind and character, no matter how well hidden. The common purpose served is that we either learn to overcome the weaknesses or we are overwhelmed by them. Few games provide such an ideal arena for confronting the very obstacles that impair one's ability to learn, perform and enjoy life, whether on or off the golf course. But to take advantage of this opportunity, the golfer must accept the challenge to play the Inner Game as well as the Outer Game.[2]

Juggling the multitude of technical and body-mind mastery skills requires that you constantly remind your inner roommate—your pesky egoic mind—that the goal is to learn your game, to practice your game, and to play your game. All that matters is what counts for your game.

The purpose of this chapter is to plant seeds and to stimulate your mind regarding the processes of learning and practice before you tackle body-mind mastery skills, technical skills, and putting it all together. Learning, practicing, and playing this game is an evolutionary, cyclic process that requires patience

---

[2] Gallwey, 8.

and perseverance. Each of us needs to be curious and to experiment to uncover our most effective and efficient learning and practicing processes. To facilitate that process and to unsettle the mind, with a view toward enabling crystal-clear thinking with respect to learning and practice, this chapter will provide information on various learning types; make some comments about awareness; offer reflections on contemplative learning; and conclude with some thoughts about possible next steps.

Learning Types

The Golf Academy of America's *Teaching Manual* outlines seven different learning types. Here is a brief explanation of each type for your reflection and perhaps experimentation to help you uncover the most efficient and effective learning style, or styles, for you.

1. Verbal or auditory: The input for the human system is hearing. These individuals like to write down what they have heard, and they frequently repeat statements to make sure they have heard correctly.
2. Visual: The input for the human system is seeing. These individuals like pictures, videos, and demonstrations, and they focus on details of body and club mechanics.
3. Kinesthetic: The input is feelings based on an awareness of the human system. These types need to perform physical, mental, and emotional activities. They normally have a high degree of hand-eye coordination, are accomplished athletes, and recall body mechanics for subconscious programming.
4. Innovative: The preferred input is personal experience to make sense of new materials. These individuals have a strong need to know why the new information is useful.
5. Analytical: These individuals have a need to know what and why the new material is important. They are normally good listeners.
6. Common sense: These folks want action and not talk.
7. Dynamic: All these individuals need is conceptual guidance before being turned loose to add personal experience to any project encountered.

A person may have a strong tendency to lean toward one type; however, he or she may draw on other types, as necessary, to learn new materials. A teacher-coach needs to become aware of and understand these types, and commit to a process that facilitates a student's learning. A student's self-awareness of how he or she best learns can certainly help the instructor optimize instructor-student time together. After working with many teachers and coaches, awareness has emerged as my best coach, and I like coaches and coaching better than teachers and teaching. Teachers tell you what they'd like to have you do: their system; coaches uncover what your desires are and help you get there.

Awareness

Awareness is what our human system experiences as we swing a golf club. Today, most golf instruction is "do this" or "do that," and the proof of right or wrong rests in an external source. Let your experiences be your proof; do not explain your experiences away. Just be with them, be patient with them, be humble about them, and do not interpret them. It is very easy to become obsessed with an interpretation of an experience and miss the experience. Interpretation merely separates us from the experience. As the Dali Lama states,

> Awareness ... means paying attention to our own behavior. It means honestly observing our behavior as it is going on, and thereby bringing it under control. By being aware of our words and actions, we guard ourselves against doing and saying things we will later regret. When we are angry, for instance, and if we fail to recognize that our anger is distorting our perception, we may say things we do not mean. So having the ability to monitor oneself, having, as it were, a second order level of attention, is of great practical use in everyday life, as it gives us greater control over our negative behavior and enables us to remain true to our deeper motives and convictions.[1]

I have learned that if I want to change something about my golf swing, the first step is to increase my awareness of the way it is. I just focus on a specific area—for example, the clubface angle at impact—and become more aware of what is there. Often our wonderful human system will self-correct—that is, get the clubface square, open, or closed at impact. Merely acknowledge

---

[1] Dalai Lama, 109.

reflections[2] in the world, receive their messages, ponder the inputs, and trust the subconscious to get the job done.

Awareness may prove to be a good teacher as you uncover how to learn most effectively and efficiently. Always be curious about awareness, because it is the primary faculty we have for knowing and learning from experience, integrating body-mind mastery and technical skills, and closely replicating play on the field of friendly strife. Our sensual experiences are the language of our neural system, which programs our muscles to provide the body mechanics that optimize club-to-ball contact at impact.

Our muscles and our minds do not speak the same language. As a result, our minds are not able to tell our muscles what to do. We need to learn that the mind is a tool to help us program our subconscious to perform; however, when it comes to performance, we must quiet our minds and trust our subconscious to perform. So just quiet your mind, and pull the trigger. Thinking merely gets in our way and becomes an obstacle to optimum performance on and off the golf course.

This awareness is nothing more than being a silent watcher of sensual inputs, thoughts, emotions, and physical sensations. Sensual inputs are processed through touching, seeing, hearing, tasting, and smelling; thoughts originate in the mind; emotions are associated with thoughts and are experienced in the body; and physical sensations are felt in the body. As noted before, if you want to change something, a first step is to increase your awareness of the way it is: just focus on a specific area and become more aware of what is there. It is always a nice feeling when our human system gets it right by not even trying.

This discussion about awareness would not be complete without a personal note. In 2001, my journey to Naropa University, Boulder, Colorado was catalyzed by the search for the connection between the mind and the body. While at Naropa, my studies included the five wisdom traditions and study abroad in Sikkim, India—both created around a core of meditation instruction and practice. At the time, the breath was the bridge between my mind and body; and today I am convinced that the breath may be the missing link between the body and the mind. However, this story is not that simple.

While at Naropa, I had three years of classes, instruction, and practice in *samatha* and *vipasyana* meditation. These two Sanskrit words capture the essence of calming meditation: one-pointedness of mind by monitoring the

---

[2] Brown, 148. Reflection as used in this book "is the occurrence of an experience in our life that reminds us of something, while a projection is the behavior that we adopt when we react to such a memory."

breath; and awareness meditation: direct personal insight, apprehension, verification, and understanding reality.

As you may have surmised, my meditation practice has continued. And it has been an interesting challenge to apply formal concentration and awareness training and practice flow to the game of golf. My experience has been that the transfer from formal, daily meditation to golf practice and play is much easier said than done. However, as discussed in Chapter 3, "Body-Mind Mastery Skills," awareness of breath, relaxed concentration, and meditation-in-action are very helpful in quieting the mind during the trigger pull for all shots as well as between shots, where tickets to insanity are readily available and where most of my golf shots are lost.

Contemplation

Another powerful learning asset for body and club mechanics is contemplative learning. After being academically immersed in the contemplative learning process at Naropa University for three years, I knew that I could uncover valuable lessons for life and golf. Contemplative learning is a natural, threefold, evolving, cyclic process: learning, perking, and meditation. First, we gather an intellectual understanding by receiving information, or knowledge, through the senses of hearing or seeing. This information is then perked: we reflect on the content of the information and explore how and whether this knowledge feels and fits with our human system. A final step is an activity, a vehicle for transformation or a practice, such as meditation for quieting, concentrating, and focusing the mind. This final step is to dwell in silence and solitude with the new information in order to gather personal insights and to experience the self in action. This has the potential to move knowledge from experience to wisdom.

An interesting pursuit might be to use golf as a practice for contemplation. Think about it: golf as practice. Golf is the yoga of the supermind, the ultimate discipline for transcendence.[3] Golf can be a practice as yoga is a practice; or golf can be a practice just as sitting meditation is a practice. Contemplation has proven beneficial in helping me learn about the inner workings of my mind and emotions, my ego, and my behaviors when stressed. It has revealed the voice of my inner roommate and can definitely facilitate my movement from reaction—$#**—to response and acceptance of things the way they are: nothing more than two consecutive shanks into the water hazard on the right, plus two lost, brand-new Bridgestone RX golf balls.

---

[3] Murphy, 53.

My recent experience with couples' golf may inspire your reflections about the wonderful game we have chosen to "enjoy," learn, and play. My wife, Cindy, and I signed up in January 2014 to play weekly in the Couples' Golf League at Sunland Springs Village, Mesa, Arizona. The games are changed each week— for example, we might play four-person best ball, with each player driving a minimum of six times; two-person best ball, in which each player must drive nine times; or two-person Chapman, in which the wife drives on even holes and the husband drives on odd holes. You get the idea: this is team effort, and egoic minds may be in control of a team's identity.

On the fourteenth hole during a round in March 2014, I was miserable and ready to quit playing couples' golf. I was in the rocks on the left side of the fairway; Cindy was in the rocks on the right side of the fairway; and the previous thirteen holes had been hard work. I was not in control, I was frustrated, and I saw no end to either the remaining holes or the subsequent rounds.

Yet that round of golf had offered some priceless information; I just needed to be ready to receive the message. That evening, while on a cross-training machine at the gym, I considered my thoughts from that afternoon. The conclusion was that the frequently recycled emotion was anger inspired by my ego. Lifting up the corner of the anger, I discovered a fear of failure, a fear of rejection, and a fear of looking bad to our opponents.

Being with the original events, perking the message, and examining my personal behavior gave birth to a renewed passion for couples' golf. These processes can enable some personal growth; it can make me a more congenial life and golf partner; they can reduce tension on the golf course between shots and during shots; and they can certainly help to reduce the number of golf shots added between holes. Moreover, this is certainly a good example of being able to transition from reacting to chaos to responding to what is present by just being with what is there. The key for me has been to go to the breath; to practice stopping when my emotions begin to trigger a reaction; and to ask the right question or questions.

- When do I get in my own way?
- Am I in my own way?
- What is my inner roommate saying?
- When did fear arise?
- What do I really want when I play golf?
- Where is the tension?

Conclusion and Next Steps

How do we learn and practice the game of golf? We are each unique and learn in different ways. Contemplative learning, mindfulness and awareness, and the psychology that augments our menu of golf technical skills can offer us the means to manifest poetic beauty on and off the golf course. According to Shoemaker, the new culture for golfers says, "There is something going on in my swing, and I must be aware of it." He continues,

> And the best way to become aware of what you are doing is not to fix it. That's right, just leave it alone for a while, stop changing it, and simply take a look at what's there ... Imagine going to the range, practicing for an hour, and not once trying to 'work on something.' Imagine a whole practice session where you simply swing your regular way and just try to feel what it is that you are doing. Imagine a practice where, for once, you don't judge yourself on the quality of your shots but on the quality of your awareness and feel. Imagine not fixing it ... simple awareness leads to consistency and improvement. I have seen it time and time again, with golfers of all skill levels. When people become more aware of key areas of their swing, their shots become more consistent. And this consistency is the beginning of great improvement. It's almost like magic. For the longest time I couldn't explain it, but I realize now that increased awareness allows the body's natural instincts to come into play, and these instincts make the swing more powerful and efficient. Awareness thus leads to improvement.[1]

Each of us needs to learn how to learn and to become aware of and understand our most effective and efficient ways of learning and practicing. We evolve our most effective modality, or modalities, by drawing on past experiences with learning and then experimenting with various ways to learn. In addition to the variety of learning modalities—visual, kinesthetic, and auditory—it is important to experiment with other techniques for learning: awareness practice; mental, emotional, and physical training and practice; contemplative training and practice; overcompensation; slow-motion practice; beginning and ending practice; partial swing practice; and imitation.[5]

---

[1] Shoemaker, 42–43.
[5] Millman, 116–29.

Needless to say, golf includes a bunch of stuff to practice. However, there are some next steps that can facilitate the learning process:

- Uncover how you can learn the game most efficiently and effectively.
- Be a good student of the game by nurturing a positive attitude. Be open to experimentation and new ideas and be willing to practice and play. When this is complemented by personal will and a passion for the game, progress is expedited.
- Learn to love the short game: it will pay dividends.
- Be curious, and experiment with the contemplative learning process. You may discover you were learning through this process without even being aware of the three levels of understanding present in the process.
- Commit to understanding and using the "awareness concept." Moreover, find a good golf instructor who uses awareness in his or her instruction. Concerning awareness Gallwey states in *The Inner Game of Golf,*

> Awareness is the primary faculty we have for knowing and learning from our experience ... an awareness instruction is an instruction to the attention to focus on a particular area for the purpose of becoming more aware of what is there ... the 'law of awareness' ... states that *if you want to change something, first increase your awareness of it.*[6]

You may want to consider starting your next practice with practicing warming up your human system for the round of challenges and opportunities that await you. This is nothing more than accepting that the human system has a need for transition, or a psychological and physical adjustment, between each ending and new beginning—that is, going from what you have been doing to the golf course for a round of golf. This adjustment is important to recognize (1) before teeing off on the first tee and (2) before each shot during the preshot routine.

- Warm up your body with some exercises.
- Warm up your mind with deep breathing and meditation.
- Check in with your static and dynamic balance.

---

[6] Gallwey, 67–68.

- Roll some putts: see, putt, and drain random lengths of up to six feet. Roll some lag putts to the green fringe.
- Using three balls for each shot, chip a few shots, and make some pitches and sand shots.
- Using a favorite iron, check your awareness and tension with a full swing.
- Using aiming stakes, make some shots to a target.
- Work through the remaining clubs in your bag, making shots to different targets.
- Make a few shots with a preshot routine for each type of shot.

Finish with a few minutes of deep breathing and quieting your mind. If you have enough time, you might want to take a short nap. Pleasant dreams, have fun, and learn as you learn best. This is your game!

Chapter 3

Body-Mind Mastery Skills

Gently close your eyes and feel the sensations of the breath as the air passes the nostrils or upper lip. The sensations of the in-breath appear simply and naturally. Notice how the out-breath appears. Or you might choose to feel the movement of your chest or abdomen as the breath enters and leaves your body.
—Joseph Goldstein

With openness, discipline, practice, and self-trust, this chapter has the potential to elevate the quality of your experiences in both life and golf. Relish this possibility: "… your mind focused on the present moment, free of concern or anxiety; your body relaxed, sensitive, elastic, and aligned with gravity; your emotions spontaneous and uninhibited … you contain the potential for body-mind mastery … a natural athlete is waiting to be born."[7] For this to become reality, we golfers just need to get out of our way. Dan Millman contends,

> Masters of one art have mastered all because they have mastered themselves. With dominion over both mind and muscle, they demonstrate power, serenity, and spirit. They not only have talent for sport, they have an expanded capacity for life. The experts shine in the competitive arena; the masters shine everywhere … Master athletes may remain unnoticed by those around them because their internal skills are visible only to those who understand. Because they do everything naturally, they don't stand out. When observing them closely, you may note a certain relaxation, an effortless quality, and a

---

[7] Millman, xiv.

kind of peaceful humor. They have no need to play a holy role. They have seen their lives upside down and inside out and have nothing left to defend or to prove. They are invincible because they contend with nothing ... Whatever they do, they practice; whatever they practice receives their undivided attention ... Body-mind masters practice everything.[8]

Mastering creative golf is unique to each person, but it certainly involves saving putts, hitting fairways, hitting greens in regulation, and consistently making ups and downs. This is a spirited challenge, and it becomes a spirited challenge squared when coupled with maintaining a low-key disposition between shots and creating a quiet mind and flowing human system that will move the clubface through the ball to the target. A nice snapshot of the second of impact might be of a personal studio where each shot is painted and brought to life on a magnificent, green velvet canvas.

As your performance, learning, and enjoyment of golf progress, your body-mind mastery—integrating your mind, emotions, and body through practice and training—evolves to become 80 to 90 percent of your game. This evolutionary journey happens as you develop the skills of meditate-in-action and of deliberately going from the conscious mind (the "inner roommate") to the unconscious mind (the "watcher"). As Bob Rotella writes in the *Unstoppable Golfer: Trusting Your Mind & Your Short Game to Achieve Success*, the ideal state of mind for each shot is to either "see it and hit it" or "see it and roll it." Learning to trust the subconscious to deliver a golf ball to the intended target is a tough assignment. It boils down to quieting your mind, looking where you want the ball to go, and reacting to the target.

Because the game of golf can be like trying to put our arms around an elephant, one task is to select carefully from a short list of simple skills that enable us to transcend to the level of the game for which we are ready. The offerings of this chapter are: (1) the cultural dilemma of treating the effects of pain and disease, as opposed to causes; (2) the opportunities presented by a marriage of 100 percent responsibility and preventive care; (3) personal experiences with body-mind mastery; (4) ideas for creating a quiet state of mind for each shot; (5) reflections on the "walk-ride" between shots; and (6) conclusions and possible next steps.

As you will note, this chapter is lengthy and may introduce concepts that are new for you. Since body-mind mastery is an evolutionary learning and

---

[8] Ibid., 165.

practicing process and is of paramount importance to your quality of life and golf, consider allowing for contemplation, perking, and experiencing time for the following sections of this chapter:

- Effects Versus Causes
- Preventive Care and 100 Percent Responsibility
- Personal Experiences
- Impact Teepee
- Reflections on Between the Shots

Consider this process for each of the sections listed above:

- Read the section's material.
- Perk the information to determine how the material fits with your experiences. You may want to consider writing about your reflections.
- Just be present with the material and begin to experience, observe, and gather insight with respect to your behaviors relevant to the material. You may want to write down your insights.

Effects Versus Causes

Sickness_____Health_____Wellness_____Well-being

The concepts of sickness, health, wellness, and well-being fit nicely along a left-to-right spectrum. At the left end is sickness, which includes addictions, allergies, afflictions, illnesses, and disease. In most Western cultures, sickness was initially subjected to the Platonic view: medicine cured maladies, and the individual had limited responsibility for lifestyle choices. As crises struck, medicine ministered to the symptoms, so prescribing pills and performing surgery created perceived cure. With the advent of the Hippocratic view, the individual assumed responsibility for his or her lifestyle and habits; and the patient began to partner with the physician. This physician, more than likely, began to recommend medicating and/or removing the effects of the perceived malady.

Because of our consumption-based mentality, health-care institutions are inspired to market and sell services and products that treat the effects of sickness, illness, and disease. These treatments are intended to facilitate the movement from sickness to health; however, many underlying causes for the pain and suffering remain untreated. Very simply, medical practice generally consists of three Rs: repair, replace, or remove.[1] In addition, because of the insatiable human demand for increased products and services, along with the associated institutional and administrative complexity, prices for health care have escalated annually.

Moving right on the spectrum, we are introduced to the idea of health. This is a condition of being sound in body, mind, and emotions. It is the condition present when an organism, or one of its parts, performs its vital functions normally or properly. Being in a state of health implies freedom from physical, mental, or emotional pain and disease. The role of the physician is to nurse the patient back to health—a state where there is no discernable illness or injury. Fundamentally, this attends to the negative effects of mental, physical, and conscious emotional experiences.

Wellness is the next concept as we move right on the spectrum. This is the point where the individual is in good health and is optimizing the physical, mental, and conscious emotional processes of living. This is a condition where the individual is beyond just healthy and is capable of maintaining the highest quality of life through accepting responsibility for self-management of the human system. Again, the role of the physician is to partner with the patient in resolving illness to a neutral point and beyond—to a high level of wellness.

Well-being is the right end of the health-care spectrum; it is the movement of an individual's health from a point of nonsickness to a state of well-being, or a high level of wellness. This involves an increased sense of personal awareness coupled with a deepening grasp of the subconscious and a new feeling of inner freedom, peace, and joy. Progressive societies strive to move individuals and the collective state of their culture from a point of nonsickness—the neutral point of no discernable illness—to a state of well-being.

The state of well-being is enabled through deep reflection on the tensions between our inner condition and our outer being as manifested in our appearance, behavior, and life experiences. In essence, we sincerely inquire about who we are and in silence and solitude listen to the dialogues we have had with the unconditioned self and the conditioned self as they have evolved. This certainly implies better lifestyle education, awareness, and understanding; moreover, it evolves the human mind from a point of addiction to a higher level that manages the causes and not the symptoms, or effects, of sickness. This is the leading edge of preventive health care and the brink of an evolution of the

---

[1] Bhaerman and Lipton, 139.

mind from unconscious reaction to conscious response to felt perception—the language of the subconscious. Bruce Lipton remarks,

> The paradigm-shattering implications of ... new science are simply this: while the immune system is the guardian of our internal environment, the mind controls the immune system, which means the mind shapes the character of our health ... programs in our mind control our health and wellbeing as well as our diseases and our ability to overcome those diseases.[2]

With the personality of our health in our individual purview, high-quality experiences with life and golf are certainly a reasonable and worthy goal. This requires wellness and implies an absence of pain and discomfort because of the effects of addictions, allergies, afflictions, illness, and disease. Moreover, this requires an unfolding surrender to our unchanging, innate selfishness and insatiable desires for more of the same. What about our immediate and near-term medical needs?

Neither the foregoing nor what follows is designed to take the place of our current health-care requirements. Even after our inner emotional discomfort begins to subside, it is important to continue medical care or seek medical care to treat the effects of our emotional, physical, and mental symptoms. For example, if we are in an automobile accident and physically injured, or if the symptoms of a diseased condition or addiction get to a point that living has become unbearable, then going to a doctor or medical specialist is absolutely necessary. These professionals know how to mend bones and sew up wounds; and they know how to control physical, mental, and emotional symptoms so we can function. Medical professionals are trained to deal with these effects; however, many of the causes remain.

As dysfunctional human beings who have individual and collective dualities—separation from others in the form of ego and identity—we have evolved to create very complex institutions and their associated institutional forces, like money, media, interest groups, and the stifling political processes. In addition are growing economic insecurities, lingering religious and racial tensions, and numerous transnational threats from terrorism to pandemic disease.

Unfortunately, these institutions include our health-care product and service delivery system, which is currently overwhelmed with administrative

---

[2] Bhaerman and Lipton, 15.

complexity and controlled by very powerful interest groups. Health-care systems are scientifically and technologically inspired; however, they are not financially motivated to share with us that our outer manifestations of unresolved discomfort—negative emotional charges, uncomfortable charges, inner discomfort, and inner dragons—within our emotional body are the cause of many diseases and illnesses that manifest in us physically and mentally. Moreover, they have chosen not to suggest that it is possible to neutralize our maladies, no matter how long we have entertained them or how acutely we have allowed them to color our life experiences. This is a nice opportunity for preventive health care to leap onto the scene and begin to enable us to manage causes.

There should be nothing more exciting than improved experiences in life and golf that reflect the peaceful and free condition of well-being, while at the same time offering extended life expectancy and collective financial incentives through reduced health-care costs and reduced entitlement taxes.

Preventive Care and 100 Percent Responsibility

In the lifelong journey of mastering the human system, a necessary step is to make an honest assessment of our body-mind reality. A subsequent step is to engage processes that can facilitate the movement of our assessed reality toward our vision of a state of well-being. For most of us, closing the gap between the vision and the current reality requires awareness, understanding, and a genuine commitment to the discipline of 100 percent responsibility and to being a student of the concept of preventive care.

Accepting the 100 percent responsibility challenge commits golfers to the principle that life and golf happen because of us and not to us. Quite simply, this concept is empowering, a way that can help produce more of what you want, and a step that has the potential to make a positive difference in arenas of your life. It certainly is a more effective approach than having a life plagued with excuses, rationalizations, created stories, blaming, justifying, and recycling the past. Of course, accepting responsibility is not a panacea. Some things are just out of our control: your golf score is a perfect example. And most of us have heard the comment "It's in my genes." The world is certainly not presented to us as vacuum-packed and wrapped in cellophane.

When we accept 100 percent responsibility, the door to health, wellness, and well-being is suddenly unlocked, and it literally flies open. The central message is this: inherent in our essence is the power to create an inner environment that is not susceptible to mental, emotional, and physical illness, sickness, and disease. In *Biology of Belief,* Bruce Lipton states,

> Thoughts, the mind's energy, directly influence how the physical brain controls the body's physiology. Thought 'energy' can activate or inhibit the cell's function-producing proteins via the mechanics of constructive and destructive interference ... The fact is that harnessing the power of the (conscious and subconscious) mind can be more effective than the drugs you have been programmed to believe you need.[3]

Concerning the dominating impact of mental perceptions of the future and the past, Michael Brown states,

> Our interpretations of what is are often deluded because they are based on what we think happened in the past and what we think may happen in the future, as opposed to what is happening right now. This is why we become so involved in the idea that we must heal ourselves. However, when we realize that all we need to heal is our experiences and then accomplish this-there is no more need for the idea that healing ourselves is required.[1]

New-edge science offers insights into healing that are evolutionary leaps, are empowering, and are an essential cornerstone for long-term health care and the wellness of our culture. Moreover, such a leap can offer high-quality health-care systems that are affordable, accessible, and cost-effective—and that include comprehensive preventive health care. This type of health care empowers us to unfold our total person and the essence of who we are: a well physical body; a bright, clear mind; a wellspring of heart-based emotional wisdom; and an unconditioned essence that energizes our chosen purposes and roles. As Lipton and Bhaerman contend in *Spontaneous Evolution,* "We humans have a lot more responsibility-the ability to respond-than we allow ourselves to believe. The programmer of the field, the genius behind the genes, is none other than our own mind-our own thoughts and beliefs."[5]

---

[3] Lipton, 95.
[1] Brown, 276.
[5] Bhaerman and Lipton, 141.

The spectrum of sickness, health, wellness, and well-being invites each of us to take 100 percent responsibility for the quality of our experiences and for the means to respond effectively to our varied and numerous life situations. Pain and discomfort and the myriad of effects of disease, afflictions, addictions, and allergies are distractions to the quality of our experiences and are a reflection of the quality of our inner being. We have a choice either to confront the pain and discomfort directly and work with causes or to employ others to treat the effects.

The October 29, 2009, issue of the *Denver Post* carried a front-page article by Jennifer Brown, "Type 2 Diabetes: Study shows weight lost is life gained," which included this:

> It seemed to Margie McCandless she was destined to have diabetes. Her mother nearly lost her eyesight because of the disease. One of McCandless' seven diabetic aunts and uncles had to have his leg amputated. Even the sugar levels in McCandless' blood pegged her as pre-diabetic.
>
> But the 74 year-year-old Broomfield widow, who participated in a 10-year study through the Colorado School of Public Health, managed to stave off diabetes-even lowered her blood-sugar levels to normal-through major lifestyle changes.
>
> The landmark study, results of which are published today in the medical journal *The Lancet*, found that people at high risk for diabetes cut their chance of developing the disease by 34 percent through weight loss, exercising five days a week and reducing fat intake. People age 60 and older cut their risk by almost 50 percent. The impact of weight loss and exercise was more profound than the most commonly prescribed drug for diabetes, which reduced the risk of the disease by 18 percent during the 10 year study ... Particularly significant, researchers said, was the discovery that weight loss, healthy diet and exercise can reduce the risk of the disease for a decade, not just a few months or years.

Yes! As McCandless attests, preventive health care and 100 percent responsibility can create an inner environment that thrives on pool aerobics, snowshoeing, and snorkeling in the Galapagos Islands. Living long and living well are not difficult. The goal is a coherence of the body, the mind, and the emotions.

Here are a few questions to initiate your contemplation period: Where have I neglected to be 100 percent responsible for my personal health, wellness, and well-being? In what areas of my life have I behaved 100 percent responsible? How has 100 percent responsibility affected me on the golf course?

Personal Experiences

The gift of our human system is a remarkable treasure that invites utmost care if we are to live and to play golf as well as we can—and if we are to uncover how good we can be. As golfers and as the programmers of what we are, coupled with having begun to perk possible changes for moving from an assessed reality to our vision of body-mind mastery, we are now in a position to consider some prescription ideas for wellness, or body-mind mastery—the foundation of quality experiences in life and golf. Here is a question for ongoing reflection about our golf: Have the pesky ego, the precision required in golf, competitive pressures, the pace of the game, or our obsessions with club and body mechanics become hindrances to performance?[6]

On a positive note, if we made some poor choices in the past, it is never too late to make the desired changes. As Peter Jacobson remarked, "One of the most fascinating things about golf is how it reflects the cycle of life. No matter what you shoot—the next day you have to go back to the first tee and begin all over again and make yourself into something."[7]

There is certainly nothing more joyful than totality manifested through a vibrant well-being that radiates coherence of mind, body, and emotions. Our wholeness and optimum inner health evolve as presence witnessing the peace of the unconditioned self and reflections in the form of messages, teachings, beliefs, and perceptions uncovered in the conditioned self—the pesky ego. We can watch our own behaviors, appearance, and unfolding circumstances. From this layperson's perspective, Lipton and Bhaerman place 100 percent responsibility and preventive health care at the forefront of attention to the self as well as to our respective roles as persons in the global community when they state,

> ... cellular citizens respond to stimuli within the body by voicing
> their opinions to the central nervous system via communications

---

[6] Gallwey, 8.
[7] DeVito, 141

that we perceive as emotions and symptoms-some of them gentle and some of them violent ... If the brain engenders wise and supportive governance, it will respond to the cellular community's feedback with leadership that offers each cellular citizen a life of healthful bliss. But, as is frequently demonstrated in our own world, if the brain is uninformed, out-of-touch, and unresponsive, it can stress a cellular community to the point of breakdown, disease, and death, which are the body's equivalent to anarchy, destruction, and warfare in civil society.[8]

For students of the dances of life and golf, an evolving prescription for preventive health care includes at least the following:

- processes for care of the physical body: exercise, balanced nutrition, restful sleep, relaxation, and listening to the body
- a layperson's awareness and understanding of the busy, pesky egoic mind and the associated emotions that trigger reflections in the world
- the means that enable us to quiet our minds and that offer insight into our egoic minds at work

Physical Body

Our physical bodies need to be refranchised, exercised, nourished, and rested. Quite simply, we have become disembodied. This implies a need to be present deliberately with our bodies and to listen to them: the tremors, the twitches, the tightness, the aches, the pains, the discomfort, and the numbness. In addition, our bodies need proper exercise[9] in the form of cardiovascular training, a program of weight training, core exercises, and stretching that could include yoga postures and connected breathing. The goal of yoga for yogis and yoginis is fourfold: to engage the physical body in movement, to increase the ability to feel movement, to reflect on the true essence of the body, and to meditate on the felt experience of the physical body and the sensations that arise.

Finally, good nutrition and a restful night's sleep are a must for our physical bodies and the foundation for our mental and emotional bodies. As the body goes, so goes the mind, the soul, and the felt perceptions; as the mind, soul, and

---

[8] Bhaerman and Lipton, 257.
[9] See Cindy Reid's *Get Yourself in Golf Shape: Year-Round Drills to Build a Strong, Flexible Swing.*

emotions go, so goes the physical body. In *Alchemy of the Heart*, Michael Brown writes, "The quality of our experiences is a reflection of the condition of our inner being. For our experiences to change, we must make adjustments at the causal point of these experiences. The causal point of all that occurs in our lives is the heart."[10] The Dali Lama offers,

> Medical science increasingly suggests that a person who is happy and peaceful, free from fear and anxiety, will enjoy tangible health benefits. It is also a matter of common sense that even people afflicted by illness are much better off if they have a positive outlook. So I consider it a simple truth that this body of ours is meant for a happy life. A happy mind is a healthy mind, and a healthy mind is good for the body.[11]

Mind, Emotions, and Ego

As much as we do not want to admit it, we are severely challenged—on and off the golf course—by the effects of a stubborn, selfish, conditioned self. As Michael Brown notes, "Even if we believe that our childhood was a good one, the nature of being born into a conditioned world means that we all had physical, mental or emotional experiences that were uncomfortable."[12] The pesky ego has been created by the mind. This development started when we were kids, continued through those early school years, and was honed as we reached maturity in our early twenties. Little did we know that the origin of suffering would be found in our mentally evolved identities. As Gallwey reminds us,

> One becomes a player of the Inner Game only when one is willing to see the existence of mental self-interference ... they only need to be open enough to admit to the presence of internal interference and be willing to employ pragmatic methods to reduce that interference ... doubt is the fundamental cause of error in sports ... When faced with the unknown or the uncertain-a common condition-human beings tend to enter a state of doubt and to tighten instinctively to protect themselves. Metaphorically, when we doubt

---

[10] Brown, 13.
[11] Dalai Lama, 27.
[12] Brown, 167.

our mental capabilities, we tend to constrict our minds or become
close-minded; when we doubt ourselves on an emotional level, we
constrict our feelings. And on the physical level, when we doubt that
we will achieve the results we want or think we may 'do it wrong,' we
tend to overtighten our muscles.[13]

Fortunately, we are also full of essential goodness. However, it can be a
lifelong challenge to chip away at the scales of the conditioned self to uncover
and unfold the beauty of our childlike, unconditioned selves. The bad news is
that our dysfunctional sides have evolved to the point where our addiction to
the mind of the ego dominates us. As with all addictions, the monopoly of the
mind is insatiable and driven by our perceived lack that we attempt to fill with
stuff from "out there": golf equipment, sex, sports, exercise, clothing, food,
movies, politics, alcohol and drugs, television, government, media, and health
care. If you can put a name on it, it will be marketed, and we will purchase and
use it to nurture the insatiable ego.

This hearty ego never gives up encouraging either more of the same or
something new to separate us from others—a fancy driver with the newest
shaft and thinnest face or that irresistible game-improvement set of irons—to
fabricate and entrench an identity, to give us more perceived control, or to
distort our perception of security. As normal, dysfunctional humans, we evolve
an ego that is sated by our addiction to the mind, and we choose to nurture
this ego because of our perceived lack. We are extremely well-trained lackeys;
we react to needs of the conditioned self because of mind-created, perceived
want. We are simply hooked! In *The Presence Process* Michael Brown contends,

> We must accept that if we are born into this world and have
> become "normal" citizens of our communities, then there is a storm
> raging within us. This is because what is accepted as normality in
> this world is a state of quiet desperation. As much as we might like to
> deny its existence, this controlled and sedated inner storm cannot be
> hidden. By gazing across the planet we can see the outer casualties of
> this inner condition everywhere. It is the storm of duality.[11]

The addicted mind is a very busy place; it seeks a tempo that desires no rest.
To test this statement, just sit in silence and listen to the voice of your mind;

---

[13] Gallwey, 40–41.
[11] Brown, 231.

and then try to quiet it. An interesting place to listen to your inner roommate is on the first tee as you are warming up to make that first drive. What do you hear being said by your conscious mind?

Working with our thoughts and the associated emotions on the golf course may be a new experience. After many years of merely reacting and not responding, we might find that a golf course poses significant challenges. We just buzz along doing, being busy, recycling thoughts and emotions, going through the motions, and replaying the past. However, to those who are open to surrendering to natural human dysfunction and to the emotional growth that can follow, a vastly expanding world can unfold, and the quality of life's experiences can become more joyful and abundant.

The task is to patiently and compassionately begin to explore our subconscious and to integrate unintegrated childhood emotions with our mental and physical wellness. This is accomplished by learning how to enter an ongoing inner journey toward mental and emotional balance. This has the potential to lead us beyond outer experiences of imbalance in a chaotic life or on-the-course situations and their associated negative emotional charges. As Shoemaker notes, we are "two shots from crazy."[15] Eckhart Tolle, in *A New Earth: Awakening to Your Life's Purpose,* contends,

> Even mainstream medicine, although it knows very little about how the ego operates yet, is beginning to recognize the connection between negative emotional states and physical disease. An emotion that does harm to the body also infects the people you come into contact with and indirectly, through a process of chain reaction, countless others you never meet. There is a generic term for all negative emotions: unhappiness.[16]

Tolle continues: "Ego-identification with things creates attachment to things, obsession with things, which in turn creates our consumer society and economic structures where the only measure of progress is always *more*. The unchecked striving for more, for endless growth, is a dysfunction and a disease."

Chipping away at the insatiable ego is a difficult undertaking and an evolving, unfolding challenge for a mentally addicted culture. However, we can embrace and be grateful for the fact that we have everything we need at our immediate disposal to uncover our individual perfection. A first step is

---

[15] Shoemaker, 4.
[16] Tolle, 213.

discovering that taking one breath at a time can truly make a difference in the quality of our experiences. A second step—or actually a monstrous leap—is recognizing and accepting that our beliefs control who we are. In *Biology of Belief*, Bruce Lipton states,

> ... the new science of *Epigenetics*, which literally means 'control above the genes,' has completely upended our conventional understanding of genetic control. Epigenetics is the science of how environmental signals select, modify, and regulate gene activity. This new awareness reveals that our genes are constantly being remodeled in response to life experiences. Which again emphasizes that our perceptions of life shape our biology.[17]

A key element of the evolving mental process is experiencing the power of our culturally conditioned ego over our behavior. Personal experience reveals that fundamental ways of showing up in the world will show up on the golf course. We just cannot hide. Western culture is addicted to the egoic mind, and as well-conditioned golfers of this very connected culture, we tote this malady into our daily lives as well as onto the practice range and the golf course.

Unfortunately, the ego enjoys being the controller of the physical body, even though it does not speak the same language as the muscles of the body. In the game of golf, a very athletic endeavor, the interfering inner roommate—accompanied by thought-associated, negative emotional charges we feel in the body—can create disaster for even the most proficient of golfers. We are not a separate self that needs constant mental attention. David A. Bhodan remarks,

> All the authentic spiritual teachers, sages and mystics have been reminding us that in reality, you are not the separate person you appear to be, but the immense ocean of consciousness in which every manifest wave of thought, sensation and experience appears and disappears in. You are the timeless and space-less capacity for all of life to unfold, including the appearance of a separate person. This non-separateness of the self and world is ultimately what all the spiritual teachings and religions point to, and this inseparably is now being confirmed by science. Modern science has proven that nothing is separate-and that each and every particle is part

---

[17] Lipton, xv.

and parcel to everything else. Everyone knows this, but has simply forgotten.[18]

The ego is nothing more than a personal identity the mind has created to separate the self from others on and off the golf course. As a result, we strive to protect this identity and lose sight of our true self. A downfall of this cultural conditioning is that we become addicted to the ego, and others see us merely as our appearance, behavior, and circumstances. Michael Brown, in *The Presence Process*, suggests that addictions are self-medicating behaviors that manifest in an attempt to sedate or control a discomfort in the emotional body. We are constantly pulling a specific outer experience into our perception because of unresolved discomfort within the emotional body.[19] Schaef and Fassel state,

> An addiction is any substance or process that has taken over our lives and over which we are powerless. It may be or may not be a psychological addiction. An addiction is any process or substance that begins to have control over us in such a way that we feel we must be dishonest with ourselves or others about it. Addictions lead us into increasing compulsiveness in our behavior ... an addiction is anything we feel we have to lie about. If there is something we are not willing to give up in order to make our lives fuller and healthier, it probably can be classified as an addiction.[20]

Concerning addicted life in the realm of the egoic mind, Tolle says,

> I don't mean to offend you personally, but do you not belong to the human race that killed over one hundred million members of its own species in the twentieth century alone? ... as long as you are run by the egoic mind, you are part of the collective insanity. Perhaps you haven't looked very deeply into the human condition in its state of dominance by the egoic mind. Open your eyes and see the fear, the despair, the greed, and the violence that are all pervasive. See the heinous cruelty and suffering on an unimaginable scale that humans have inflicted and continue to inflict on each other as well

---

[18] Bhodan, 1–2.
[19] Brown, 56.
[20] Schaef and Fassel, 57.

as on other life forms on the planet. You don't need to condemn. Just observe ... That is insanity.[21]

The challenges of the mind that we golfers face are many. David A. Bhodan writes,

> What you are the mind can never know. What you are produced the mind. How can that which is produced perceive its producer? The problem is, you think you are the mind. The mind can never perceive the Perceiver–that which is Seeing. Not knowing its limits, the mind keeps trying to find its Source, to no avail ... Human beings are wired in such a way as to place attention on all the thoughts, sensations, feelings and experiences that come and go, instead of finding out who it is that is experiencing all of that. As a result of being focused on the 'outer world' of events, we often find ourselves tormented and confused by what happens to us. Not knowing who we really are, we invariably suffer. Granted, our lives have happy and joyous times, too, but pain and suffering is usually right around the corner.[22]

A man once told the Buddha, "I want happiness." The Buddha replied, "First remove 'I,' that's ego. Then remove 'want,' that's desire. And now all you're left with is 'happiness.'" This is a difficult challenge and requires that one begin to acknowledge our infinite reflections in the world.[23] The world offers flawless feedback; and this feedback is our interpretation of the world as seen, heard, tasted, touched, smelled, and thought. This interpretation is energized by self-created beliefs, concepts, and patterns that have become the mind of the ego and associated emotions. With respect to positive, neutral, or negative interpretations, we have a choice. However, most of the time we react to feedback, not making a choice; choice implies deliberate response to feedback, or reflections in the world.

Here's a good question: who is in charge of the decision to either react or respond? The ego, or the inner roommate, takes control of reaction; the self is in charge of the response. As Tim Gallwey said, "I am convinced that the happiest and best golfers are those who have realized that there is no single

---

[21] Tolle, 110–111.
[22] Bhodan, page before preface.
[23] Brown, 142.

gimmick that works and that good golf is attained only by patience and humility and by continually practicing both Outer and Inner Game skills."[21]

Gallwey certainly suggests that tips and listening to the tipsters will not get the job done. A few baby steps that can move us forward are to accept 100 percent responsibility for our well-being; to surrender to and accept the reality of our human imperfection; and to evolve a learning process and practice that identifies outer and inner skills that work for us on and off the golf course. The challenge for each of us is to carve out a journey that fosters a calm state of mind, coupled with a solid purpose and high-quality connections built on a foundation of compassion—a virtue that appears to have eluded many.

An obvious question is "What does this all have to do with golf?" With a happy life comes happy golf, and with happy golf comes a happy life. *Being present* with a golf ball, a golf club, and a target on a golf course can offer numerous lessons about connections and relationships. The quality of our experiences with others and the impact of the golf club with the golf ball require a unique, clear, and quiet state that implies pure engagement and complete commitment to being present in the moment. Perhaps this state is pointing us in the direction of genuine happiness, and it appears to speak loudly about a purpose-driven life as it models the way for us as persons, in our relationships, and when skillfully enabling and serving others. Bountiful health, wellness, and well-being targeted at a sense of balance for our human system, complemented with a learned and practiced capacity to listen to and watch our minds and emotions, seems to carry a message that one needs only embrace golf and life, as they unfold, to garner a happy life and golf game. There are no magic formulas! Dan Millman suggests,

> Meditation practice-whether sitting, standing, or moving-develops insight into the process of your thoughts. By paying attention in this way, you recognize, acknowledge and accept thoughts and feelings, but no longer let them drive your behavior or run your life. This is the beginning of body-mind mastery. The first step to transcending the mind is to notice how you blame external circumstances for your anger-to understand that the problem lies not simply in the circumstance but in your mind's resistance to *what is.*[25]

---

[21] Gallwey, 13.
[25] Millman, 40.

James Gimian remarks,

> So often we find ourselves at the limits of our ability to be open
> and compassionate in our day-to-day world, right here, right now.
> When we can bring our attention and loving kindness to those very
> ordinary, difficult moments-not run away or cover them over but
> just be there with them-then we are bringing genuine meditation
> practice into our life.[26]

Ask this question to initiate your contemplation period: How is my inner
roommate treating me on the golf course?

Meditation

Yes! We can uncover a process that will help us quiet our monkey mind
and reopen our innate awareness. This can become reality through numerous
meditation techniques that include connected breathing and the experience
of present-moment awareness, where life happens moment to moment. Pure
joy, abundance, and glowing health can unfold as we begin to experience an
authentic, unconditioned well-being: we become conscious of our consciousness
and begin to trust the creative subconscious mind, and we see ourselves as we
are, as opposed to what the mind's eye and the world would like us to be. We
can literally begin to be nothing more than our awareness.

Consider selecting a good meditation instructor to support learning one-
pointed concentration and awareness. These two qualities are a natural fit
for the game of golf. The sport offers unlimited opportunities to practice
one-pointed concentration and presence with every shot; and it offers an
opportunity for meditation-in-action and the acknowledgment of reflections
between shots, where the golfer spends most of his or her time during play.

What inner roommate stories do you plan to listen to during your next
round of golf? Fears? Feelings? Judgments? Aches and pains? Tight muscles?
A sore wrist? An aching lower back? A tender rotator cuff? If you are open to
learning and input, each story can offer a fascinating message and an insightful
glimpse of a storied past.

With continued, disciplined practice of meditation, you will be able, at will,
to prepare your studio for an optimum golf shot with mere presence and *silent
space*. Some of the skills that can be available are as follows:

---

[26] Gimian, 144

- Connected breath that facilitates one-pointedness of mind and relaxation as you prepare to begin your routine and take a shot.
- An evolving capacity to de-clutter the mind as you begin a chosen preshot routine.
- A growing ability to create a heartfelt visualization of a desired shot.
- One-pointed concentration, at will, to facilitate trust of the subconscious as you pull the trigger on every golf shot. This is nothing more than pulling the trigger and swinging the club without thought, though it's easier said than done!
- An enhanced, optimum flow of power with a relaxed, supple body at the point of impact of the clubface through the ball to the target.
- An authentically joyful response to the beauty of the sculpted shot—a Tiger Woods or Rory McIlroy fist pump.
- On the course and off the course: insight into the egoic mind, its demons, and the associated behaviors that we express through body, speech, and mind. We can learn to be our own watcher and develop an ability to listen to our inner roommate.

Through mindfulness and awareness practice and training, we are able to evolve to become on-the-course masters of presence and silent space for the optimum execution of a purposeful golf shot that places the ball in the fairway, on the green, or in the hole. Moreover, these learned and practiced skills embrace human spirituality and are expressed by each individual in creative, effective, and helpful action in a world where our global neighbors have become quite close. Sakyong Mipham Rinpoche remarks, "It seems we all agree that training the body through exercise, diet, and relaxation is a good idea, but why don't we think about training our mind? Working with our mind and emotional states can help us in any activity in which we engage, whether it's sports or business or study-or a religious path."[27]

An addiction to ego can manifest itself in you being plagued on the course and at practice by an untamed mind that is intent on directing the muscles in how to hit a golf ball. The expertise of your mind can help you determine *what* needs to be done in the game of golf; however, you must trust your properly programmed body with the *how* of rhythmically delivering your clubface through the ball to the target. Your ego-mind merely interferes with your efforts to deliver tension-free body mechanics for optimum contact of the club head with the ball at impact. Bob Toski remarks,

---

[27] Sakyong Mipham, 13.

> The reason we make free arm movement on the practice swings
> but not on actual shots is because our mind does not trust our body
> in situations that really matter. We feel we must dictate to our body
> or it will let us down and embarrass us. So the mind doesn't work
> with the body as a team-they are not as one-but rather it overrules
> what the body wants to do-and can do-naturally.[28]

Consequently, mental skills development must commence with tools directed at quieting your culturally conditioned ego-mind. You need to be able to draw on the knowledge resources of your mind when necessary and to quiet and clear your mind when it is time to pull the trigger and deliver the clubface through the golf ball at impact. Developing these mental skills requires intent and commitment:

- to be awake and to carry this presence into everything you do;
- to be watchers of thoughts, emotions, and physical sensations;
- to not create tension by recycling negative thoughts and emotions;
- to be a golfer, a good caddy, and a resident psychologist;
- to be open to exploring the menu of contemplative practices and experiences; and to reflect on these questions: Why do I play golf? What is the purpose of golf? What is my grade as a playing partner? Am I present when standing with the golf ball, the target, and the club?

Meditation can evolve into meditation-in-action, the journey, and the destination. This awake state reveals itself to others as behavior: a pleasant smile, a consoling touch, helping others, holding a door open, and humbleness or an act of kindness on the fairway, on the green, or at the first tee. It is also the ability to engage totally and to receive every situation exactly as it is, without preconceptions or judgments. As good human beings, as well as golfers, we grow to embrace difficulties, deep sadness, upset feelings, and injustice while staying aware, present, and available.[29]

Here are two questions for your contemplation period: How can meditation help my golf? How many different forms of meditation practice are there?

---

[28] Love and Toski, 100.
[29] Shapiro and Shapiro, 100.

Impact Teepee

"The golf swing is like sex. You can't be thinking about the mechanics of the act while you are performing."
—Dave Hill

For every shot, we need to evolve a routine for creating a personal teepee where our minds become clear and quiet[30] and the programmed subconscious is given absolute trust to deliver an unleashed, earth-shattering impact through a golf ball bound for a visualized target. As the legendary Bobby Jones remarked in 1929,

> The golf swing is a most complicated combination of muscular actions, too complex to be controlled by objective conscious mental effort. Consequently, we must rely a good deal upon the instinctive reactions acquired by long practice. It has been my experience that the more completely we can depend upon this instinct-the more thoroughly we can divest the subjective mind of conscious control-the more perfectly we can we execute our shots ... That intense concentration upon results, to the absolute exclusion of all thoughts as to method, is the secret of a good shot ... After taking the stance, it is too late to worry. The only thing to do is to hit the ball.[31]

Turning off the conscious mind is a skill that a coach is not able to teach you. A coach can point to the moon, but all golfers need to uncover their unique means to create the clear and quiet state of mind and react to the target or trust the subconscious to execute the shot.

If you conceptualize that your mind has an inner roommate who pesters and a watcher who is the sentinel, in a state of relaxed concentration[32] your inner roommate is absent and your watcher is present and abiding. This is the natural state of the subconscious, and, for golfers, it is important to grasp that concentration of thought cannot occur unless the watcher has learned and practiced guiding the flow of thought. This practice includes taming the monkey mind, quieting patterns of interference, committing to learn and feel

---

[30] Shoemaker uses "clear and quiet state of mind" in *Extraordinary Golf*. This concept has also been referred to as relaxed concentration (Gallwey) and flow state (Csikszentmihalyi).
[31] Gallwey, 19–20.
[32] Ibid., 169–185.

the subtle variables of club and body mechanics, and trusting the watcher to perform. As Gallwey reminds his students, "… learn to be aware and let go at the same time."[33]

In regard to creating a clear and quiet state of mind while standing poised over a golf ball, Michael Lardon, author of *Finding Your Zone: Ten Lessons for Achieving Peak Performance in Sports and Life*, offers exceptionally poignant and wise advice and counsel when he states,

> Getting into the Zone is less about what you do in the moment; it is more about what is done long before the competition. The overarching goal is to develop mastery of your mind, like the samurai swordsman.[34]

A tough assignment is to learn and practice creating solitude and silent space, in which you trust the subconscious to visualize the target and hit a ball to it. My first "not thinking while swinging" experience occurred several years ago on the practice range of Heritage @ Westmoor Golf Club, Westminster, Colorado. At the time, my awareness was focused on distracting my conscious mind while I swung a seven iron. My techniques included listening to "The Impossible Dream"; counting one on the backswing and two to trigger the forward swing; playing "fi fi fo fum" in my mind; and Gallwey's "Da-da-da-da" and "Back, Hit, Stop."[35] All of a sudden, I became aware that my mind was totally distracted and I was just hitting golf balls to a target without thinking about my body and club mechanics. Tim Gallwey states,

> The ideal state of mind for a golfer executing a shot is the "zone." This is a place where the supple body and the supple mind are synchronized; thinking is not required. Golfers in the zone feel that their conscious mind is separated from their body and subconscious mind; and they feel they are sitting in the stands watching their physical body perform. This state implies the body is on auto pilot and the senses are wired directly to the subconscious brain. These senses embrace the fairways, the greens and the targets. The golfer reacts without conscious thought and awareness. When the shot is

---

[33] Gallwey, 185.

[34] Lardon, 143. Consider studying this research-based work that offers concise, clear ways to realize your best performance.

[35] Ibid., 24–25.

done, the golfer has trouble remembering exactly what transpired. However, an errant shot can quickly move stellar performance to sub-par performance because the mind begins to tinker with thoughts, analysis and reasons what went wrong as a second shot is shanked out-of-bounds … How do we return to the zone? One can only create the preconditions for going into the zone, i.e., the golfer is not able to deliberately move to the zone, but can make it more likely to happen. A state that is possible to create is a clear and quiet state of mind. This state is different because it is deliberately created. In the zone requires no conscious effort. A second difference is that with a clear state of mind the golfer's awareness of the target is more embellished than when in the zone.[36]

How does a golfer create a clear and quiet state of mind? Each of us needs to evolve our unique method. Here are some experiences from my evolving process:

*Stand behind the ball and in clear view of the target.

- Go to the breath—deep breath in, long breath out—and continue to focus on the breath.
- Commence clearing the mind and begin releasing detected tension.
- Make an efficient and effective estimate of the situation: lie, weather variables, green conditions, hazards, etc.
- Select a club.
- Identify a relatively small target, and creatively visualize the shot required.

*Move to the ball and set up.

- Continue to focus on the breath, relaxing the physical body, and clearing and quieting the mind.
- Rotate the head, with eyes along the target line, for a final glimpse at target; return the eyes to the ball and narrow the focus to a dimple on the ball.
- Concentrate on a clearly chosen object while maintaining a soft focus on the target.
- On the out-breath, unconsciously react to the target.

---

[36] Ibid., 76–77.

Bob Rotella offers,

> You look at the target, and then your eyes come back to the ball. You surrender to what you see. You surrender to your talent, your skill. You trust your body will do what is necessary to send the ball to your target. You surrender to your subconscious and you accept that if you do that, you have your best chance to make the ball go where you have looked ... There is a spectrum of states in which a golfer's mind can be ... The ideal state of mind for a golfer executing a shot ... is the "zone" ... its brilliant, it's enticing, but it's elusive ... In golf, the zone is a place where body and mind are perfectly coordinated and thinking is not required ... golfers in the zone feel that their conscious mind is detached from their body and subconscious mind. They have a sense they are watching their bodies do amazing things ... The eyes take in the fairways, the greens, the You are concentrating on one thing. It is the ideal condition for good golf. The zone is associated with starting to think about results ... You cannot make yourself get into the zone. But you can create the preconditions for going into the zone ... getting your mind into the next-best state ... the clear and quiet state ... identify a target and envision the shot ... clear your mind, switch off the conscious brain, and unconsciously react to your chosen target. There are two differences between this state and the zone. The first is the conscious effort you made to get there-in the zone, there is no conscious effort. The second is that you're more aware of the target than you would be if you were in the zone ... But this clear-and-quiet state is still a very good place to be when you're playing golf ... Having the mental discipline to keep a clear-and-quiet mental state even when things are not going well is a hallmark of an excellent golfer.[37]

Harvey Penick, a legend of golf teaching, remarked, "All seasoned players know, or at least have felt, that when you are playing your best, you are much the same as in a state of meditation. You're free of tension and chatter. You are concentrating on one thing. It is the ideal condition for good golf."[38] Gallwey contends,

---

[37] Rotella, 74–79.
[38] Parent, 3.

There is one *master skill* underlying the myriad of specialized skills required to excel at anything. I call it "relaxed concentration," and I call it the master skill because with it one can learn to improve any skill, and without it, it is difficult to learn anything. It is not easily defined or taught, but it can be learned and even successfully coached. Everyone has experienced the state of relaxed concentration at one time or another during moments of peak performance or experience. In those spontaneous but all too elusive moments of heightened alertness and perception, actions seem artlessly excellent and life seems simple and whole. Even in complicated, demanding situations, the effort needed is clear and actions flow out of us that are uncannily appropriate. Golf shots are made as if they were the easiest ones imaginable, and we wonder what we ever thought was difficult about the game.[39]

The purpose of this section has been is to offer some key fundamentals for just being present right here, right now; just being here with whatever is happening, as opposed to being someplace else because we are distracted by the world out there. Being here, right now, facilitates the opportunity to create an in-the-flow experience when you are present, in your space with the ball, the club, and the target, ready to pull the trigger to impart an earth-shattering clubface blow to an innocent, awaiting golf ball, sending it off to the intended target. It should be fairly easy to make an estimate of the situation, select a club, and identify the required target. Visualizing the shot and the golf techniques will take some coaching, practice, and on-the course play; and my experience shows that clearing the conscious, busy mind and quieting the conscious brain requires instruction and ongoing practice. Rotella suggests,

> Golfers, to play their best, have to have the mental discipline to turn off their conscious brains just when the analytical portion of their minds tells them there are a dozen compelling reasons to turn the conscious brain on ... Good golfers need to keep the target as part of their mental equation and react unconsciously to the target. You are looking for a soft focus on the target, not a hard focus. Take a casual look at it. Make the target small, but not too small that you have to squint to see it.[10]

---

[39] Gallwey, 171–72.
[10] Ibid., 68–71.

Gallwey states, "Concentration of thought cannot occur unless the thinker has learned to direct the flow of thought, slow it down, and, possibly, bring it to a stop."[11] Practice creating your unique teepee on every shot by doing the following:

- Breathe and draw upon skills learned to quiet your mind using a process that works for you.
- Identify a relatively small target and become enchanted with it.
- Visualize the shot, and emotionally and sensually embrace the target.
- Quiet your mind and commit to feeling one key variable of either the set-up or full swing. Some examples of key variables are static and dynamic balance, smoothness of takeaway, completion of backswing, quality of transition from backswing to forward swing, and stability of the right side (for right-handed golfers) during the shoulder turn and shoulder tilt.
- React to the target: see it and hit it; or see it and roll it.

Bob Toski comments in *The Touch System for Better Golf,*

> A key skill is learning to quiet an interfering mind while trusting the subconscious mind to swing a golf club as it has been trained to do. Win the inner game to win the outer game: the inner game is always being played; the outer game is only played during each shot that must have a purpose that is executed in the present moment with awareness, intent and trust.[12]

Here are two questions for your contemplation period: How quiet is my mind when setting up to hit a golf shot? What could I do to improve my ability to quiet my mind, on call?

Reflections on Between the Shots

The purpose of this section is twofold: (1) to share why our human tendency on the golf course is to have reflections that either offer incorruptible feedback or generate upsets that put us on the brink of insanity and wasted shots; and (2) to share possible avenues to confront our reactions to these feedback

---

[11] Gallwey, 174.
[12] Toski, 103.

opportunities, thus improving our enjoyment, performance, and learning both on and off the golf course.

Two Shots from Insanity

A nice place to begin is with my recent, on-the-course experiences that have revealed much during my time between shots. The first learning is that eighteen holes of golf is a very stressful, tension-filled experience. For many of us, our tendency is to collect and store tension across the shoulders, in the nape of the neck, and in the hips. While sitting in a lounge chair, watching television the other evening, I noticed that the right side of my neck was tight and sore. I applied some Arnica gel and became curious about what may have caused the discomfort. With continued massage, the muscles on both sides of my neck were very tender.

Another eighteen holes the next day, coupled with the previous night's awareness, revealed that the muscle tension started to appear on the fourteenth green. As soon as the stress was detected, my solution was to go directly to deep breathing. The tension began to melt, and it was present neither on the eighteenth hole nor during the evening spent in the lounge chair, reading a book.

About three weeks ago, during a round of couples' golf, I was miserable. The game my wife and I were playing was alternate shot. We were all over the course and were having to make shots that neither of us had ever made before. Even though our scoring was not horrible, my mind, speech, and behavior were making life miserable for both of us.

Later that afternoon, on a cross-training machine at the gym, I was reflecting on the miserable day at the golf course. As I pondered my behavior, it dawned on me that between shots I was reacting to and recycling all the chaos and misery I was creating because of our errant shots. The message was that I needed to respond to the chaos, not react. Playing couples' golf with my dear wife had been a nice messenger, and I was open to receiving its message. The next round with my wife will determine how good the student has been. It may take a few rounds and a dose of patience to detect reduced tension and a lasting change in behavior.

Three months ago, during a round of golf with my wife, my son, Doug, and his girlfriend, Soojin, it dawned on me on the thirteenth tee, as I was going through the numbers, that I was bored. I had no passion; each shot was a real drag; scoring was hard work; and it felt like the round would never end. Regarding falling asleep on the course, Coop and Wiren write,

'I just fell asleep out there' is a phrase club golfers and tour players alike use to describe certain indifferent rounds that are the result of under-arousal. One way to prevent an excess of such indifferent play is to occasionally remind yourself that it really doesn't take much more time or effort to try to do it right than it does to perform indifferently. This attitude of giving every shot its best possible chance to succeed is certain to result in better shot making and in greater personal satisfaction.[13]

As soon as I realized what was happening, it was clear that this was certainly not the first time it had occurred. As I was standing there on the thirteenth tee, my immediate response was to go to the breath and be in my own space for a couple of minutes. As I launched my preshot routine, new energy was unleashed, the drive was wonderful, and a birdie on the par five hole was deserving of celebration and a nice fist pump.

The first tee on a round of golf has been a fascinating playground for my inner roommate. This morning the couples' golf game was a shotgun start, designated driver, each player needing to make nine drives, followed by two-person best ball to the hole. Since my wife was traveling, my partner was Joyce, and we were playing with Gertrude and Hap. I had met Joyce before, but had never played golf with her. My first meeting with Gertrude and Hap was the first tee. And my inner roommate was busy:

> *Need to relax and get off to a good start with a nice drive. Don't want to embarrass myself. It will be interesting to see how Joyce hits the ball. Did I make a good decision by agreeing to play with her? Wow! Gertrude is really skinny. She must be sick. Hope she is okay. Hap sure is a grouchy, bossy old fart. He really treats Gertrude poorly. She cannot do anything to please him. Should be an interesting round of golf.*

Aside from all the inner chatter, judgments, and ego rambling, the round was fun, and my partner and I played well. Hap and Gertrude struggled. I learned about awareness and listening to my inner roommate, and I laughed at the chatter of my conscious mind. It would be fascinating to experience the chatter of others' minds on the first tee. However, this is certainly not my film. I have more ego stuff to see, feel, and hear than I need.

---

[13] Coop and Wiren, 140.

Watching personal thoughts, emotions, and behaviors during pace-of-play activities can also be a fascinating experience. What are your thoughts and emotions about you own pace-of- play? What does your inner roommate say about your playing partner's pace-of-play? How about the group in front of you? Any thoughts about the group behind you? What goes on when you need to pick up your pace? What goes on when your group is falling behind and a playing partner says your group needs to pick up the pace?

Pace-of-play was abruptly brought to my attention on March 23, 2013: hole one, a par four, Sunland Village East, Mesa, Arizona. The remark about my putt for a birdie was, "That sure took a long time." This statement caught me by surprise and fired my rockets. By the time my par putt dropped into the hole, I was fuming and regretfully unleashed a string of expletives. On the second tee, I apologized for losing my cool.

In that event, the statement, "I don't mind what happens," did not work. My mind recycled the event for several days. What was under this anger? Why the destructive criticism about my pace-of-play? Anger? Competitiveness? A twosome on the second tee was waiting for a foursome to tee off on the par three. No one, including the foursome behind us, was going anywhere.

All ego, just ego, more ego! Golf is part of my current identity, and trampling this ego stirred its defenses: fear of imperfection in the eyes of the beholders; fear of rejection by the provider of warm fuzzies. Is it possible to make changes to personal pace-of-play and not interfere with gaining and maintaining presence with the shot: the target, club, ball, course, and body? Yes!

On a recent round it felt like the SkyCaddie was playing distance games. After a change of batteries, the distance challenges and frustrations continued. Inside, I was smokin'. On the sixteenth hole, a long par three, the drive was a tad long, in the rough, and to the right of the green. The SkyCaddie offered fifty-six yards to the hole; my estimation was thirty-five yards to the hole, and intuition told me to pace the distance to the hole. My choice was to forgo pacing off the distance.

I was frustrated with the distance disparity, and my chosen shot was a fifty-six-yard pitch shot with a sand wedge. The shot was beautiful, over a playing partner's head and over the green. Now the ball rested twenty yards to the left of the green and in the rough. Next was a chip shot that went to the fringe of the green to the right of the hole. Three more putts, and it was a triple bogey! But there had been at least two wasted shots, perhaps three. With a final round score of seventy-four, two holes had accounted for five wasted shots because of recycled frustration with a SkyCaddie. Insanity? Yes! And all between shots.

Here is a question for your contemplation period: What does my between shots, inner roommate chatter sound like?

Tickets for Release from the Asylum

My ticket master is meditation-in-action. Meditation-in-action is just being present: watching the breath, chanting a favorite mantra, walking mindfully, or feeling grateful for things around me. All are ways of bringing the distracted mind into just this moment. It may not be possible to maintain it all the time in our daily life, because there are endless external distractions—let alone the inner demands of the ego and ongoing mental chatter. But we do not have to let such distractions rule.

As we cultivate mindfulness, we naturally see the ongoing movie in our minds and are less likely to be caught up in the storyline. Each time we are pulled into dramas and self-centeredness, we can stop, bring our attention back to the present, and rest in that awareness. Fred Shoemaker remarks, "I find that very few golfers actually stay awake for an entire round. They seem to "check out" at many points along the way. Instead of noticing what's happening around them-being extrospective-they go back inside their heads and experience their same old stuff."[11]

The "same old stuff" Shoemaker refers to is his concept of introspection: judgments, evaluations, and the desire to look good and to have approval; self-doubt, excitement, hope, fear, and thoughts about the perfect swing. Here is a really helpful discussion of the inner thought process, as described by Life Coach Charles Pacello:

> Our thoughts are neither good nor bad; they just are what they are. It is only the meaning we give to them that makes them so. Metaphorically, our thoughts are like cloud forms passing through the sky. If your mind is like the sky, and it is, when it is clear, it is vast, infinite, peaceful, and bright. When clouds appear, these are like our thoughts, and they will pass through as long as we don't attach ourselves to them.[15] The problem is when we have storms in our lives, we attach ourselves to the storms, and these storms become cataclysmic because we won't let go of them. They will

---

[11] Shoemaker, 56.

[15] Ringu Tulku Rinpoche, a spiritual teacher, once remarked in a seminar, "The sky is always there. All one needs to do is clear the clouds."

pass, if we just let them go. But we don't, and so we stay in the storm long after the storm has passed. We keep reliving the storm repeatedly, trying to stop it, trying to bring some kind of resolution to it, trying to do something different so the storm doesn't hit, but all we do is perpetuate the consequences of the storm. The recycled storm disrupts our lives, influences our decisions and choices in the present, and we live out our lives trying to make up for what happened in the storm that is long gone. As Plato says, "What is once done, can never be made undone," however, what we can do is change our thoughts about the things that have happened to us, remember who we are, reconnect to our true selves, learn and grow from the mistakes of our past, make peace with those who hurt us or who we may have hurt, recontextualize and reframe the story of our past to find the good that came out of those experiences, heal our past, and then, take those lessons from those traumas and build a better, healthier, and happier future.

I want you to imagine your mind is like a projector of a movie and your thoughts are the images and words coming across the screen. These words and images will continue on past as long as you decide not to hold on to them. If you hold on to them, they will give you all the emotional charge, both positive and negative, attached to those images, however, if you just let them pass by, they lose their power over you. Now, let me ask you something, does the movie screen hold on to the film image? No, of course it doesn't. Now consider this: you are the projector of all those thoughts running across the screen in your mind which are then reflected back to you in the outside world. So, what are you going to do? Don't hold on to your thoughts. Return to the present. Be in the present moment. The only place where any of this exists anymore is in your mind.[16]

As golfers, we are a mere two errant golf shots from internal chaos, whether we like to admit it or not, or perhaps because we are numb to the experience. This inner mental and emotional turmoil may evolve to become a trip to the golf asylum: a frustrating round of golf with substandard performance and a lost opportunity to learn and grow. In *Extraordinary Golf: The Art of the Possible*, Fred Shoemaker writes, "… no matter where they are on the golf course, most

---

[16] Pacello, a one page reflection paper used with the 11-29-14 permission of Charles Pacello (www.charliepacello.com.).

golfers are always two shots away from being crazy. No matter how well they're playing, a couple of bad shots in a row can change their entire experience. They are always on the verge of being upset."[17]

Let's take a look. Yesterday was a gorgeous day: sunshine, beautiful green grass, a slight breeze with the scent of cut grass, two great playing mates, and a new driver to christen. As I teed off on hole one, I had the normal desire for others' approval, coupled with typical predrive judgments and evaluations about everyone about to scurry off to chaos. Absent any preround warm-up, the first drive with the new driver went better than expected. The next shot, a four iron, found a lower branch on a nearby tree and plopped to the ground, well short of the green.

Perhaps this mishap was an omen of insanity; it quickly ended the mantra of "greens in regulation." My mental tune changed to "up and down," and my focus was on the next shot: distance to the six-foot circle around the cup, club selection, swing mechanics, routine, visualization, and the intimidating lateral water hazard between the ball, the green, and the cup.

The six iron was the perfect club, and I decided to shank the next two shots into the lateral water hazard. Now lying five, the threshold of crazy was crossed, and commitment to the insane asylum appeared like a reasonable end. The sixth shot bounced on the green and came to rest on the fringe, waiting for two putts and a snowman for the scorecard. The remainder of the round was frustrating and miserable: a seven, two pars, and the rest bogeys, all producing a resounding forty-four.

If any of this story sounds a wee bit familiar, Fred Shoemaker really makes the solution sound simple. He says, "By focusing your attention on real things and not on your internal dialogue, your mind will begin to calm down."[18] For my egoic mind, hitting the tree and shanking two iron shots into the lateral water hazard felt real, especially according to the relentless pandering of my mind and associated emotional chaos. The certain result was insanity and a less-than-satisfactory, unenjoyable round of golf. I did not want to be on the course.

As I reflected on this round of golf, there were some nice lessons: do not play golf to please others; go to the course early enough to allow for a good warm-up before teeing up the ball on the first tee; and let go of the inner roommate dialogue created by errant golf shots—sure tickets to insanity.

Experience says that at the end of nine holes of good golf, the mind easily thinks, *Gosh, it would be great to have such great success on the second nine holes.* Peter Huber and Dave Hockett, instructors at The Golf Academy of America, would

---

[17] Shoemaker, 3.
[18] Ibid., 5.

always ask us this question: "What happened when you made the turn?" A frequent, frustrating experience is a completely unfocused tee shot on the 10th tee. Just yesterday, hunger and thirst were a real issue: all I needed to refocus was something to eat and a drink of water. Also, I noticed the absence of deep breathing. Of significance was what I learned to take to the next 18 holes: do my best, breathe deeply, quiet the mind, and let go of what I am not able to control.

Since we are human, and some of us have chosen to play the game of golf, a foregone conclusion is that on the golf course—and most likely during the course of our lives—our reflections of the world energize upsets. At times we become irritated, impatient, attached, angry or maybe even deluded. For most of us, feedback stirs the mental and emotional process of our egoic mind and can cause less-than-desirable performance and behavior on and off the golf course. In *The Unstoppable Golfer*, Bob Rotella writes, "... golf gives a player incorruptibly honest feedback."[49] The challenge is to receive the feedback and to learn and grow from this exemplary gift.

The goal of acknowledging feedback is to improve our quality of life by responding to people, objects, events, and places, as opposed to reacting to the thoughts and associated emotions, words, and behaviors they catalyze in our physical system. Our target is perception of the world: to adjust our view of the world and thus our outer interaction with it. Quite simply, this becomes an alteration of our attitude about the causes for the effects of thoughts, words, behaviors, objects, and places. Our challenge becomes accepting 100 percent responsibility for our quality of life: life happens because of us and not to us.

As many of us know and perhaps have experienced, we have a choice about whether to react to feedback or respond to reflections. Of course, good feedback requires celebration and warm fuzzies; however, mental and emotional reactions to negative feedback are sure tickets to a cycle of mental and emotional chaos. An unemotional response to those errant, unsuccessful golf shots permits us to quickly learn, grow, and release the experience. Bob Rotella states, "It's important to let yourself rejoice in good shots and accept unsuccessful shots phlegmatically. Too many players do the opposite. They get angry at unsuccessful shots. They regard great shots with no emotion, as if great shots were as unremarkable as a bus arriving on time."[50] Gary Wiren says, "In fact, golfers may lose more strokes in between shots, by mis-thinking and

---

[49] Rotella, 2.
[50] Rotella, 27.

mis-feeling, than they do actually swinging the club, and it is mainly because of the special challenge the excess amount of time places on them."[51]

The self-created mind of the ego, or our inner roommate, is the culprit that offers reflections of the world. As we move through life, seeing, hearing, touching, tasting, smelling, and thinking are food for decisions, evaluations, and judgments. During our early years, the human system we live with today began to take shape. Although the emotional, mental, and physical elements of this system were growing in parallel, the emotional system was the first priority, followed by the mental and physical parts of the system. During this development process, we made decisions that became the foundation of attitudes, beliefs, and concepts that gave rise to our ego: the mental perception of who we think we are, which is a far cry from who we really are.

One of our early discoveries was that we could behave in ways that rewarded us with praise, recognition, and positive judgments. For many of us, the keepers of these warm fuzzies were Mom and Dad, along with teachers, ministers, brothers, sisters, and classmates. Early in life, we began to concentrate on having the approval of others, and this behavior remains with us today. We are still trying to please Mom, Dad, and a long list of lifetime enablers. That poor shot on the golf course would have made Dad unhappy. This can give rise to an upset and unleash the inner roommate to work on tarnishing our self-image. Since we get what we think about, that next shot is displeasing too. Perhaps a second shank into the lateral water hazard is just what the shot doctor ordered. There is a dose of incorruptible feedback in that shank, and it has lessons waiting for us. It is full of wisdom.

Let's take a look at how we might open the door to this valuable feedback. As we have evolved, causes and their associated effects on the human system began to separate. A consequence is that we are able to react as either victims or victors when thoughts and their associated emotions are triggered. Because of pauses between cause and effect, it never occurs to us that we are actually complaining about ourselves and the consequences of our own actions or that we are actually competing with ourselves because of obstacles that we have placed in our own way.

The initial step of the acknowledgement process is to identify the messenger. For example: today at the gym, the television was too loud. Directly, the messenger was the television set; indirectly, it was the woman who turned up the volume in order to hear *World's Funniest Videos* while she exercised on a machine that was three cardio machines removed from the television set. This situation was irritating and distracting; and the theme of my ego's inner dialogue revolved around her

---

[51] Coop and Wiren, 58.

discourtesy and lack of respect for others. It felt like the situation was being done to me, not because of me. My ego was in the role of the victim of her behavior, and I eventually put the thoughts on a bus to Tucson.

Ask this question during your contemplation period: What are your tickets for release from the asylum?

Conclusion and Next Steps

As you move forward with life and golf, as you ponder causes and effects, 100 percent responsibility, preventive health, and possible body-mind mastery "action plans," here are some possible next steps:

- Consider using golf as a practice. It can become a field of very friendly strife.
- Use connected breathing to relax and facilitate concentration.
- Practice concentration, meditation, and contemplation.
- Target for a good night's sleep. It is always critical for optimum performance.
- A well-balanced diet can improve energy levels and attitude.
- Put together a plan for regular, targeted physical exercise. Cardiovascular training; power and endurance exercises; and stretching to help flexibility and prevent injury to your core muscles, shoulders, wrists, and lower back. Exercise can also boost your attitude and motivation, ease stress, and soften anxiety.
- Practice going to the breath. The regulation of the connected breath, combined with good set-up and concentration, can facilitate a release of tension to create a good shot at impact.
- Learn to sense static and dynamic balance at the point of origin, or centering point, one to one and a half inches below your belly button. As mentioned before, without a good sense of static and dynamic balance, learning additional body and club mechanics skills is not possible.
- Evolve the means to build a teepee for each shot that creates a clear and quiet space in which to trust your subconscious to perform as it has been programmed.

- Between shots, practice meditation-in-action. Tim Gallwey contends that "the walk between shots is one of the most critical parts of the game."[52]

Golf mirrors life and offers a wonderful opportunity to learn some of life's curriculum on a field of friendly competition. It is not possible to "hide" on the golf course: we show up on the golf course as we show up in life. Moreover, as with life, the process of golf includes ups and downs and provides infinite learning opportunities about both golf and life. As with life, the journey of golf is the destination. A nice place to start is with a vision of the future in mind; and then walk, one step at a time, from current reality toward your vision. Here is a sample to get you inspired and energized to create a personal vision.

Golf Vision

Golf is a "practice," a process, and a mystical experience. Golf is my actual experience when I play and practice. Standing in the future, this is how I want my life and golf to be: a vision that inspires and enlivens; a journey that is the destination; and a trek that is alive with possibility. This is just starting with the end in mind: I played the game as well as I could play it; and I found out how good I could be.

- Breath control.
- Accept what happens with grace and maturity.
- Keep all possibilities open.
- Have meaningful, energizing relationships and conversations. Remember: extraordinary minds talk about concepts and ideas; average minds talk about events; and small minds talk about people.
- Create each shot in the silence and solitude of your personal studio with a conscious use of skills, talents, and creative imagination; get immersed in the game.
- Play your game and trust the subconscious to perform.
- Be conscious of fears, feelings, distinctions, and "going through the motions."
- Awareness is an excellent way to learn and practice.
- Have a relaxed warm-up time and process.
- Practice what counts, and optimize learning through awareness and instinct.

---

[52] Gallwey, 12.

- Have equipment that fits and feels good.
- Create and use effective exercise, concentration, meditation, and contemplation processes.
- Get good rest and eat healthy foods.
- Target for minimum intensity between shots and for a low level of importance for each shot.
- Learn and enjoy with tension-free performance; scores will be what they are—not controllable.
- Model the way: as a person, in relationships, and when enabling others.
- Seek peace of mind coupled with purpose, intent, and connections founded on compassion.
- Be remembered for integrity and a rock solid code of personal ethics.
- Do not lie, cheat, steal, or abuse sex, alcohol, and drugs.
- Be humble, optimistic, considerate, courteous, grateful, and appreciative; create a strong self-image and respect others.
- Get out of your own way; manage thoughts and emotions.
- Golf is an expression of who you are: experience what is really happening.
- Embrace chaos and learn to dance with it.
- Love the short game.
- Become a body-mind master who stays in the moment.

Masters of one art have mastered all because they have mastered themselves. With dominion over both mind and muscle, they demonstrate power, serenity, and spirit. They not only have talent for sport, they also have an expanded capacity for life. The experts shine in the competitive arena; the masters shine everywhere ... Master athletes may remain unnoticed by those around them because their internal skills are visible only to those who understand. Because they do everything naturally, they don't stand out. When observing them closely, you may note a certain relaxation, an effortless quality, and a kind of peaceful humor. They have no need to play a holy role. They have seen their lives upside down and inside out and have nothing left to defend or to prove. They are invincible because they contend with nothing ... Whatever they do, they practice; whatever they practice receives their undivided attention ... Body mind masters practice everything.[53]

---

[53] Millman, 165.

Body-mind mastery, health, wellness, and well-being are concepts that continue to fascinate scientific, objective, and subjective minds. Just walking down streets and seeing fellow humans provides evidence that society's health could certainly use more attention. As Plato once remarked, "The great error in the treatment of the human body is that physicians are ignorant of the whole. For the part can never be well unless the whole is well." As golfers, our assignment is to accept 100 percent responsibility and to recognize that inherent in our essence is the power to create an inner environment that is not receptive to disease and illness. If our fortunes mean we have disease or illness, we need to find a good physician who will partner with us and enable us to return to a state of no discernable sickness. When we are physically, emotionally, and mentally capable, we are on our own to maintain our highest quality of life, stay out of our own way, and play and practice great golf. Hit 'em high and straight, and practice those inner and outer skills and three-foot putts.

CHAPTER 4

Technical Skills

For paying and playing members of modern golf, the plethora of technical skills and technology definitely nourishes insatiable addictions and obsessions with body and club swing mechanics. The inner roommate thrives on pestering with "do this" and "do that"; the marketers beckon us to a constant feeding frenzy using all the various media available; and the numerous technological advancements available in the golf industry invite us to invest in their secrets to uncovering the magic of a perfect golf swing.

A conceivable vision for students of the game is that they have access to a golf technological institute that would enable them to uncover their individual learning styles through a long-term, direct experience of a full menu of available training aids. These training aids could offer the students direct feedback about a desired motion; and through the process of awareness, it could offer students the means to program their muscles to perform consistently that motion. As with any training aid, it is imperative that the students be present with the feedback and not merely move through the motions. This also requires a sincere commitment to long-term practice.

Being aware of feedback is a learned skill that originates with the common human purpose of awakening, or becoming aware of the separation of thoughts from our awareness. As development of this skill progresses, we are able to allow the awareness to flow to our "doing activities." A good example of a doing activity is learning a correct golf motion through effective, timely feedback from training aids like Dynamic Balance System (DBS), SAM PuttLab, MEGSA Perfect Practice Equipment, or TrackMan golf radar.

The Dynamic Balance System is appealing because it enables an aware student to feel both static and dynamic balance. Good balance is one of the most important skills for the golfer to learn because it contributes directly to performance, enjoyment, and learning. Until a golfer is able to sense static and dynamic balance, he or she is not able to make a consistent, controlled golf motion. Without this ability to sense balance, the 1,500-plus repetitions required to learn a proper motion and to program the muscles to perform the motion subconsciously are a waste of the student's time and effort.

I have not used SAM PuttLab, but the system appears to offer good feedback on twenty-eight of the most important parameters of a putting stroke. On the surface, this is too much feedback for a golfer. My interest is in simplicity; the goal is to enable a person to put the ball in the hole. For me, putting is about speed and direction: look, set up, dance, look, connect the breath, and go. The Coutour system is simple, and it works for me: eyes over the ball; sense static balance; and gently grip the putter as the trailing arm hangs comfortably from the shoulder.

MEGSA Perfect Practice Equipment looks complicated, and I have not used it. It appears to offer excellent feedback for sixteen elements of the swing motion. Providing the element selected to practice is the one that corrects the many, it could get the subconscious programmed and the muscles trained with the required 1,500 repetitions of a proper motion. A nice feature is that the equipment integrates the club mechanics and the body mechanics required to execute the proper motion.

In the hands of an experienced, professional, and passionate golf coach, TrackMan golf radar has the potential to enable a committed golfer to function better on the course, to enjoy the game more, and to learn an exceptional amount about ball flight and club data. My TrackMan experiences at The Golf Academy of America and at PING Golf club fitting have been excellent.

These training aids certainly have accuracy, flexibility, and reliability. However, a student of golf can quite easily become distracted and not learn basic technical skills, and the shoulds and should-nots can put us on a path of complexity. An alternative when learning the golf swing is to develop your own swings. Tim Gallwey suggests,

> This is done by paying attention to certain critical swing variables without trying to make any changes. Change takes place as a spontaneous result of increased awareness-at whatever level of proficiency your swing may be. Technical knowledge can be used to

identify which critical variables to observe and to give a hint about
the direction of change that might occur.[1]

The desired results for this chapter are certainly not to enable golfers to
become technical gurus. The materials are designed to offer technical golf
swing fundamentals that "can be used to identify which critical variables to
observe and to give a hint about the direction of change that might occur."
These basics can create a foundation on which you might be inspired to become
a true student of the game, to perform better on the course, to practice more
effectively and efficiently, and to enhance your enjoyment of the game. You
will discover that the following materials can also be excellent guides when
you need to review golf swing fundamentals for a particular type of golf shot.
It is important to recognize that detailed information on the "how" of club
and body mechanics, ball position, routines, and ritual is absent. That detailed
instruction is better obtained from personal experience, professional golf
instructors, pertinent golf literature, and other sources you determine are best
for your particular type of learning.

The offerings in this chapter are golf's logistical factors, ball flight laws,
and fourteen principles that impact the logistical factors of the golf ball.
The discussion will then move to some coaching goals coupled with a basic
delineation of "what" is required in relation to club mechanics, body mechanics,
ball position, routines and rituals for putting, the short game, scoring wedges,
and the full swing.

Logistical Factors

The two logistical factors for each golf shot that require consideration are
direction and distance. Direction involves the right or left accuracy of shots,
or how far left or right of target the ball is or will be. Distance involves how far
the golf ball has traveled, or how long or short the ball will be in relation to
the chosen target.

---

[1] Gallwey, 119. Golfers interested in learning more about inner swinging are invited to review
and study chapter 8, "Inner Swinging," 117–43, in W. Timothy Gallwey, *The Inner Game of
Golf* (New York: Random House, 1998).

Ball Flight Laws

The ball flight laws reflect the physical forces of nature, and they work every time, without fail. At the moment of impact, the ball is not affected by swing style, but rather by purely functional phenomena. Here are the five laws:

1. Speed of the club head at impact: impacts distance
2. Angle of approach of the club head to the ball: impacts distance
3. Centeredness of impact of the club head with the ball: impacts distance
4. Face angle of the club head in relation to the ball-target line: impacts direction
5. Path of the club head in relation to the ball-target line: impacts direction

If you'd like additional information on ball flight laws you can explore these absolutes in the introduction to *Practical Golf* by John Jacobs (New York: Lyons Press, 1989).

Fourteen Principles

Before offering a brief look at the fourteen principles, two introductory comments are needed:

• When ball flight is incorrect, it most likely was a result of poor set-up, because that is the cause of 85 percent of errant ball flight effects. Set-up involves stance and weight distribution, ball position, posture, and muscle readiness.

• When working with club and body mechanics, a certain principle is probably the cause of a ball flight effect. For example, distance can be reduced when the left arm of a right-handed golfer is bent on take-away and forward swing, because the width of the arc of the arms and club is less than optimum, resulting in a less than optimum centrifugal force of the club head on impact with the ball.

The following fourteen principles are mechanical elements of the golf swing that can help solve distance and direction issues. They have a direct relation to and a significant influence on the laws, but require a golfer's, coach's, or teacher's subjective judgment with respect to applying the mechanics to the swing.

Direction Influences

- Grip: The placement of the hands on the golf club. This is the connection of the golfer to the golf club. The grip is open, closed, or neutral.
- Aim: The alignment of the clubface and body in relation to the target.
- Position: The relationship among the back of the leading forearm, wrist, and hand at the top of the back swing. The wrist is either flat, cupped, or arched.
- Swing plane: This "pane of glass" matches the path of the club shaft; this is the tilt and direction of travel of the inclined plane that is made by the shaft of the club as it moves through the backswing and the downswing.
- Release: The return of the body, arms, and club head to a position that is similar to their starting position; this allows energy that was created during the back swing to be released through the club head to the ball at impact.

Distance Influences

- Width of arc: The amount of extension of the golfer's hands away from the center of rotation during the swing.
- Length of arc: The total distance the club head travels during the back swing and forward swing.
- Lever system: The levers formed by the lead arm and the club during the back swing; hinging the wrists and positioning the club shaft approximately ninety degrees to the leading arm. Cocking occurs on the backswing and uncocking/release occurs on the forward swing.

Distance and Direction Influences

- Connection: The positioning and maintaining of the various body parts in relation to one another in set-up and during the swing; maintaining the shoulders, hands and golf club triangle; parts working together. This is very important during transition from the back swing to the down swing.

- Set-up: A combination of foot placement, ball positioning, body posture, muscular, readiness and weight distribution.
- Timing: The combined sequence of the movement of the body and the club to produce an efficient result; synchronized body and club mechanics.
- Swing center: The point between the top of the spine on the back of the body and the top of the sternum on the front of the body.
- Dynamic balance: Maintaining balanced body control during the swing as the golfer transfers weight from the trailing foot to the leading foot, and maintaining balance while in motion. Transferring weight properly is a prime component of a productive golf swing. Even before other elements, developing a proper weight shift with balanced body control is paramount.
- Impact: The moment of truth; striking through the ball with the center of the clubface with as few compensating moves as possible.

Another term discussed is *preferences*. Preferences constitute a third level of priorities in establishing a golf swing. They are important because this is the level at which we most often practice and play. Having a preference is the act of choosing a particular approach, method, device, etc., over all others. Examples of preferences are chipping ball position and stance. Two personal preferences for chipping are the ball position being even with the heel of the right foot; and the stance being open with both feet.

Coaching Goals

- To be centered, to be aware, and to feel static balance during set-up. The static balance point is approximately one and a half inches below the belly button.
- To feel and maintain dynamic balance: stability of lower body; legs remain flexed; head remains relatively steady; and during body motion note how the dynamic balance point remains relatively stable at a point approximately one and a half inches below the belly button.
- To have coordinated movement during take-away and to transition from the backswing to the downswing.
- To move the club to the top of the backswing without hurrying.

- To attack the ball, hit through the ball, and stay with the ball through impact.
- To target for consistent timing (the parts of the swing are connected and synchronized); to find a personalized tempo (the rate the in-swing moves); and to find a rhythm that is fluid and smooth.
- To learn to feel each swing. Experience shows that learning the overall feel of an effective swing programs the subconscious: this programming is conducive to replicating a swing time after time.
- To learn to be present and watch the sensual perceptions, thoughts, and feelings. Practice not nurturing the pesky dysfunction of the egoic mind. As performance, enjoyment, and learning of the game progress, body-mind mastery evolves to become 80 to 90 percent of the game.
- To uncover how we learn best and to have practice that integrates skills and closely replicates on-the-course play. Awareness is the best teacher and is the power that is concealed in the present moment. It is the primary faculty we have for learning from experience. Experiential, kinesthetic sensations (seeing, hearing, feeling, and touching) are the language of the muscles that provide the body mechanics that optimize club-to-ball contact at impact. If the golfer wants to change something, a first step is to increase his or her awareness of the way it is: just focus on a specific area and become more aware of what is there. If something is awry, there are many times when our human system will self-correct. Contemplative learning can also be a powerful asset: hear or read information; perk it; and sit with it in silence and solitude to move the knowledge to experience.
- To have practice priorities: body-mind mastery skills, putting, short game, scoring wedges, full swing, and course management.
- To have restful sleep, to eat well, and to exercise daily. A good night's sleep is critical for optimum performance; a well-balanced diet can improve energy levels; and regular, targeted cardiovascular training, coupled with power and endurance exercises and stretching, can boost attitude and motivation, ease stress and anxiety, and prevent injury to vulnerable muscles of the core, shoulders, wrists, and lower back.
- To have equipment that fits and feels good.

Club Mechanics, Body Mechanics, Routine, and Ritual

The purpose of this section is to offer simple golf fundamentals commencing with putting. Subsequently, the fundamentals will progress to the short game (chipping, pitching, and sand play) and scoring wedges. Finally, the power game clubs will be introduced: long irons, hybrids, fairway woods, and the tool of choice for the teeing ground, the driver.

You will note very soon that many fundamentals become repetitious as your knowledge of the game progresses. For each of the elements of the game, five topics will be noted: club mechanics, body mechanics, ball position, routine, and ritual. Here are some definitions:

- *Body mechanics*: A physical motion of a swing that creates club head speed, face angle at impact, flight pattern, carry distance, trajectory, and back spin.
- *Club mechanics*: A physical motion of the golf club: the grip, the shaft, and the club head. The visual and felt physical phenomena of a golf club's grip, shaft, and club head.
- *Routine*: Assessing the shot conditions, visualizing the entire shot, and feeling the swing.
- *Ritual*: A personal trigger that commands/releases the subconscious to perform as it has been programmed. Webster's says that a ritual is practice done or regularly repeated in a set, precise manner so as to satisfy one's sense of fitness; often felt to have a symbolic or quasi-symbolic significance.

As you begin to explore each of the coaching strategies, it is important to keep in mind that playing good, consistent golf requires experiential knowledge. The golfer needs to have the information, perk the information, begin to gain knowledge, and move the knowledge to wisdom on the course. Have fun, learn, and perform to the best of your ability. Good golf evolves one step at a time.

Coaching Strategies

Putting

Quite simply, putting is about line, speed, and stroke; it contributes 40 to 45 percent of the shots made during a conventional round of eighteen holes of golf. Putting requires a delicate balance between inspired creativity and applied science. I certainly do not pretend to be a putting guru, so I recommend you seek advice and counsel from your chosen experts. My putting has profited a great deal from several sources:

- Todd Sones, Coutour Golf
- Peter Huber, Gary Balliet, and Ed Ekis, instructors at The Golf Academy of America
- *Dave Pelz's Putting Bible*
- Dr. Joseph Parent, *How to Make Every Putt*
- Dr. Bob Rotella, *Putting Out of Your Mind*
- Ed Shoemaker, *Extraordinary Golf*

Dave Pelz is the putting technical guru, and *Dave Pelz's Putting Bible* offers the golfer an exceptional amount of data, guidance, advice, counsel, and wisdom with respect to putting. His "Fifteen Building Blocks of the Putting Game"—aim, path, touch, rhythm, ritual, feel, face angle, stability, attitude, routine, putter fitting, power source, impact pattern, flow lines and green reading—are based on research and practical application, and they provide plenty of information for the technically minded golfer. You may find green-reading, the fifteenth building block, useful as you begin to refine your ability to master green reading and to trust your subconscious to deliver the correct speeds and distances for your putts.

After you have had some preliminary instruction for putting, it is important to find a qualified club fitter who can work with you to properly fit the length, lie, loft, and grip size of your putter. This is a fairly easy process that should take approximately thirty minutes and will prove beneficial as your skills progress. As you begin the putter selection process, you need to move forward with correct club specifications, good feel, and gut instincts. Now, let's take a peek at some basic mechanical skills for putting.

- Club Mechanics
  The goal of putting mechanics is to have control of the ball's speed and direction. There are generally three requirements for a putter to get the ball in the hole: clubface alignment, the path of the club, and the contact of the clubface with the ball. At impact (1) the clubface must be perpendicular to the desired ball to target line; (2) the path of the club should feel natural and free, be pendulum-like, and replicate

a swinging screen door; and (3) the contact of the sweet spot of the clubface must be through the ball and with the equator of the ball.

- Body Mechanics
  - Set-up (GASP)
    - ✓ Grip: Both hands act as a single unit; not too loose, not too tight; palm of right hand and back of left hand face target and are parallel.
    - ✓ Aim: Parallel left of ball to target line.
    - ✓ Stance: Feet a comfortable distance apart, fourteen to sixteen inches. Feel static balance: Toes and heels should not be able to leave the ground.
    - ✓ Posture: Turn forearms, tuck elbows, and tilt spine forward for comfort.[2]
  - Swing Motion
    - ✓ Single lever: With good setup posture, the club, hands, arms, and shoulders move as a coordinated unit—a triangle that pivots at the swing point just above the breast bone.
    - ✓ Triangle: Left shoulder, right shoulder, hands-grip-putter; sensation of natural and free pendulum; conscious of freedom of upper arms from the sides of the upper torso; swinging screen-door path; motion is smooth and silky.
- Ball position: Experiment starting with one ball forward of center of stance. Note: consider marking the diameter of the ball with a line to facilitate putter face aim and alignment.
- Routine
  - Read the green with horizontal, binocular-like vision that programs the subconscious to deliver the right direction and speed.
  - Visualize the shot required.
  - Make rehearsal swings, as necessary.
  - Sense the touch and feel. Touch programs the subconscious for the "what" direction and speed required for the putt. Feel senses how the "how" muscles are to perform to produce the required putt.
  - Move to ball and set up: eyes over ball; back hand swings freely to putter grip; feel static balance (the toes and heels are not able to leave the ground); and release detected tension.

---

[2] Todd Sones, Coutour Golf.

- Ritual
  - ○ Pull the trigger. "Conscious breathing stops your mind."[3]

Short Game

The short game and putting account for 60 to 65 percent of the shots made during a conventional round of eighteen holes of golf. In this book, the short game consists of chipping, pitching, and sand shots. The goal of the short game is to save putts by placing shots within six feet of the hole. Knowing distances for various short game clubs is critical for short game success and improved scoring. Learn to love the short game.

- Chipping
  Chipping is used for shots that are off the green and normally twenty or fewer yards from the hole. The golfer normally chooses to chip the ball when putting is not possible.
  - ○ Club Mechanics
    - ✓ Single lever swing motion.
    - ✓ Triangle: Left shoulder, right shoulder, hands-grip-club; freedom of upper arms from the sides of the upper torso.
  - ○ Club selection: Pick a target on the green, three to four feet from the fringe; use the lowest trajectory club that will hit the target and roll the ball to the hole. Typical clubs from which to choose are the 5, 7 or 9 irons, PW, and SW; other clubs can be used: putter,[1] hybrid, 3 Fairway Wood, and GW. Experiment with clubs that work for you. Practice direction, distance, and air time/roll time with your favorite clubs. Target for having the ball go either into the hole or within a three- to six-foot circle around the cup. Practice until you have ten consecutive balls either in the cup or within the three- to six-foot circle around the cup. Thicker grass requires higher lofted clubs and a ball position that is back in the stance. Target for no grass between the clubface and the ball; and pay particular attention to the club path to ensure the clubface moves along the desired ball to target line. If you choose to use a fairway wood, a hybrid, or longer irons for regular chipping, consider

---

[3] Tolle, 246.

[1] D. Pelz, "The Chiputt" in *Dave Pelz's Short Game Bible: Master the Finesse Swing and Lower Your Score* (New York: Aurum, 1999), 219–20, 8.11.

marking the chipping length of these clubs with a piece of tape wrapped around the shaft. For consistency of swing mechanics, my preference is to have all wedges the same length.

- ○ Body Mechanics
  - ✓ Set-up (GASP)
    - ➢ Grip: Experiment to discover what works for you. Same as putter, overlapping, interlocking, or ten-finger; both hands act as a single unit; not too loose, not too tight; palm of right hand and back of left hand face target and are parallel; wrists cocked down to facilitate not getting "handsy" and to prevent hitting the ground with the heel of the clubface at impact.
    - ➢ Aim: Face and body aligned parallel left of ball to target line; clubface aligned perpendicular to ball to target line.
    - ➢ Stance: Feet six to eight inches apart; feel static balance.
    - ➢ Posture: 60 to 65 percent of weight forward on left. Note: tip toward target after other parts of set-up are complete. Choke up on grip to point where grip meets shaft; hands in front of left thigh. Visualize pulling the club through.
    - ➢ Wrists are cocked down to facilitate having relatively firm wrists and a steady triangle; toe of club touches ground, heel of club off ground; with the ball back, ball is long gone before a "chunk" can occur.
  - ✓ Swing motion: Smooth, rhythmic, finesse, maintain triangle, free arms from body swing; no flip; swing left arm and club as a unit; back and forward, brush the grass; slightly descending, crisp impact; little ball before big ball; follow through, moving straight down the line through impact; 20 percent of backswing for follow-through. No grass between ball and clubface.
- ○ Ball position: Experiment by starting with center of stance; try front of right toe before opening stance twenty degrees by rotating on heels; ball is now off of right heel.
- ○ Routine
  - ✓ Shot required.
  - ✓ Club selection.
  - ✓ Visualize shot and pick a close-in target three to four feet onto green.

✓ Rehearsal swings, as required.

✓ Sense touch and feel to program the subconscious.

✓ Move to ball and set up; create silent space. Note: eight seconds max from start to pull of trigger.

  ○ Ritual: Trigger for smooth, flowing stroke. "Conscious breathing stops your mind."[5]

- Pitching

Pitching is shots of thirty yards or less to the hole. The golfer normally chooses to pitch when the ball cannot be putted or chipped and/or there is an obstacle between the ball and the hole that needs to be negotiated with a shot that has a high trajectory. For example, shooting over a green-side bunker. The goal of the pitch shot is to have the ball finish inside a six-foot circle around the cup. Knowing club distances is critical to an effective pitch shot.

  ○ Club Mechanics: Club selection is based on ball-to-target distance. The four key club variables required to produce the desired shot are as follows: (1) the clubface angle must be perpendicular to the ball to target line; (2) the club path must be parallel to the ball to target line; (3) contact with the ball needs to be centered on the clubface; and (4) the angle of attack needs to ensure that the golf ball is struck before the ground is struck and the divot is created. Remember little ball first; and hit down to hit up.

  ○ Body Mechanics

    ✓ Set-up (80 to 85 percent of effective shot)

      ➤ Grip: Neutral.

      ➤ Aim: Parallel left; intermediate target; align clubface, then align feet; open left foot thirty degrees.

      ➤ Stance: Heels twelve to fourteen inches apart; feel static balance; feel and release tension.

      ➤ Posture: Relaxed, free of tension.

    ✓ Swing Motion: Synchronized, finesse swing;[6] hips follow shoulders; smooth, dead hands swing; clock system[7] for controlling distances with the back swing; take-away is critical; follow through to show heel of right foot, club over left shoulder. Finesse swing is upper body, no torque; lower

---

[5] Tolle, 246.

[6] Pelz, 62–78.

[7] Recommend the "clock system," *Dave Pelz's Short Game Bible*, 88–102.

body follows shoulders. Feel dynamic balance: timing, tempo, rhythm; feel and release tension.

- o Ball Position: Centered between heels. Note: error toward right heel, not more than one ball.
- o Routine: Visualize shot; select club; practice swings, as desired; select a close-in target, move to ball, and create silent space.
- o Ritual: What is your trigger to commence the swing?
- o Drills
  - ✓ Practice finesse swing in front of mirror; just let the body swing naturally: hands, arms, and body; feel hips follow shoulders.
  - ✓ Swing the club and feel the club head; hit a few balls for five minutes for fun.
  - ✓ *Know distances!* Note: Accuracy is not a significant issue for pitch shots; the key is distance. How far do you hit each of the wedges from 7:30, 9:00, and 10:30? Write these distances down and eventually tape these distances on each of the wedges.
  - ✓ Start learning and practice the 9:00 finesse swing; move to 10:30; and finally, 7:30, the toughest part of the clock system to learn.
  - ✓ Practice fifteen-yard pitch, twenty-yard pitch, and thirty-yard pitch. Goal: every shot in the six-foot circle in order to save putts.

- • Sand Shots
  - o Club Mechanics: Do not limit sand shot club selection to the sand wedge; the club selected drives distance control. Use all irons and know their respective distances from greenside bunkers and fairway bunkers. Remember not to ground the club in the sand. Fairway bunker shots require that the ball be placed back in the stance to help ensure the club strikes the golf ball before it hits the sand. Placing the ball back in the stance requires selecting a club of greater loft, because the club is delofted when the ball is placed back in the stance. Because the ball is back in the stance, take a couple of practice swings to help ensure the clubface follows the desired ball-to-target line. For greenside bunker shots, the clubface is open to forty-five degrees, measured from the ball to target line, and normally the club grooves follow a line drawn from the ball to target line to front of the left foot.
  - o Body Mechanics

    ✓   Set-up:

        ➢   Grip: Neutral.

        ➢   Aim: Left of target two to three paces. Experiment with this aim point and make calibrations, as necessary.

        ➢   Stance: Anchored, open stance; feet fourteen to eighteen inches apart.

        ➢   Posture: Relaxed, free of tension; 60 percent of weight on left leg; tilt toward target when ready.

    ✓   Swing Motion: All greenside bunker shots are made with the 9:00 finesse swing because the desired distance is established by the club selected. Fairway bunker shots require a full swing, and for these shots it is critical to square the clubface to the ball to target line before take-away.

    ○   Ball position: Forward off inside of left heel for greenside bunkers; back in stance for fairway bunker shots. For greenside bunkers, the club enters the sand at the low point of the finesse swing. Experiment with two to three inches behind the ball. This entry point will differ based on the texture of the sand: wet, dry, fluffy, deep, etc.

    ○   Routine: Visualize shot; select club; practice swings, as desired; select target on the green and in the sand; move to ball; and create silent space.

    ○   Ritual: As mind becomes quiet, pull the trigger.

Scoring Wedges

Scoring wedge shots are thirty to one hundred yards from the hole. Knowing the respective club distances is critical to an effective scoring wedge shot. The goal of a scoring wedge shot is to have the ball finish inside a six-foot circle around the cup.

- Club Mechanics: Club selection is based on ball-to-target distance. The four key club variables required to produce the desired shot are (1) the clubface angle must be perpendicular to the ball to target line; (2) the club path must be parallel to the ball-to-target line; (3) contact with the ball needs to be centered on the clubface; and (4) the angle of attack needs to ensure that the golf ball is struck before the ground is struck, and the divot is created.

- Body Mechanics
  - ○ Set-up (80 to 85 percent of an effective shot)
    - ✓ Grip: Neutral.
    - ✓ Aim: Parallel left; intermediate target; align clubface, then align feet; open left foot thirty degrees.
    - ✓ Stance: Heels twelve to fourteen inches apart; feel static balance; feel and release tension.
    - ✓ Posture: Relaxed, free of tension.
  - ○ Swing Motion: Synchronized, finesse swing; hips follow shoulders; smooth, dead hands swing; take-away is critical; follow through to a high finish, show heel of right foot, and finish with club over left shoulder. Finesse swing is upper body, no torque; lower body follows shoulders. Feel dynamic balance: timing, tempo, rhythm; feel and release tension. Remember to maintain a wide arc with your left arm.
- Ball Position: Centered between heels. Note: error toward right heel, not more than one ball.
- Routine: Visualize shot; select club; practice swings, as desired; select a close-in target; move to ball; and create silent space.
- Ritual: What is your trigger to commence the swing?
- Drills
  - ○ Practice finesse swing in front of mirror; just let the body swing naturally: hands, arms, and body; feel hips follow shoulders.
  - ○ Swing the club and feel the club head; hit a few balls for five minutes for fun.
  - ○ *Know distances!*

Full Swing

A full swing is normally used for the driver, fairway woods, hybrids, long irons, and scoring wedges when a full swing distance is required for a shot. The full swing has the following components: take-away, back swing, transition, forward swing, impact, and follow-through.

- Club Mechanics: Club selection is based on ball-to-target distance. The four key club variables required to produce an ideal desired shot are (1) the clubface angle must be perpendicular to the ball to target line; (2) the club path must be parallel to the ball-to-target line; (3) contact with the ball needs to be centered on the clubface; and (4) the angle of attack needs to ensure that the ball is struck before the ground is struck and a divot is created. Moreover, the angle of attack for a driver will normally be ascending at impact. It is important to grasp that an ideal swing is not probable and that there are many variations of the full swing, along with weather and course variables, that can move a ball to a desired target.

- Body Mechanics
  - Set-up: Be consistent, stable, centered, and free of tension; be aware of and feel static balance; detect and release tension.
    - ✓ Grip: Comfortable; grip must return club square to the ball; grip is open, closed, or neutral. Left hand: place the club so that the shaft is pressed up under the muscular pad of the heel and also lies across the top joint of the forefinger. The main pressure points are the last three fingers and the heel pad. The V created by the thumb and index finger should point to the right eye. Right hand: A finger grip. The shaft should lie across the top joint of the fingers, definitely below the palm. The two middle fingers apply most of the pressure. Practice with your thumb and the forefinger off the shaft. The V of the right hand points directly to your chin. Both hands should work together as one unit. The little finger of the right hand locks into the groove between the forefinger and big finger of the left hand. The left thumb should fit snugly into the cup of the right palm. Experiment with various styles of the grip and choose a grip that works for you.
    - ✓ Aim: Body aligned parallel left of ball to target line.
    - ✓ Stance: Comfortable, approximately shoulder-width apart.
    - ✓ Posture: Forward tilt; comfortable, allows full shoulder turn and shoulder tilt.
  - Swing Motion: Anchored right side; full shoulder turn; shoulder tilt; swing back, make a smooth transition, swing through, and stay down with and through the ball. Attack the ball at impact; divot in front of the ball. Maintain the width of arc and tempo; target for vertical stability of the swing center and make a full follow-through. Be centered, feel dynamic balance, and maintain relative stability of lower body. Have coordinated movement during take-away and

coordinated transition from backswing to downswing; target for consistent timing, tempo and rhythm.

✓ Take-away: Smooth and fluid; swing away from ball; coordinated movement of hands, wrists, arms, feet, knees, legs, hips, and shoulders.

✓ Backswing: Turn shoulders (approximately ninety degrees) and hips (approximately forty-five degrees); upper-body motion is around the axis of the spine; the shoulders tilt. Keep a flexed right knee throughout the backswing. This permits wind-up, resistance, and transition into the forward swing for release of full power at impact; target for a stable lower body, firmly planted feet, and a relatively stable swing center. There is no hurry in completing the back swing. It is more important to have the club in proper position at the top of the backswing than to be in a hurry to put the club at the top of the swing.

✓ Forward swing: Transition starts naturally with a reflex action of the right knee, legs, and hips moving toward the ball, before the backswing finishes; the weight shifts to left foot; the torso and shoulders resist as the arms and hands are pulled down by the legs, hips, and back inside the target line. Initiate the forward swing by turning your left hip and right knee to the left, while at the same time delaying your arm and hand swing. Target for coordination of your body and club mechanics while sensing and maintaining dynamic balance: this equates to timing.

- Ball Position: Varies by club. Tee the driver off the inside of your left foot; fairway woods and longer irons forward of center; hybrids and shorter irons toward center of stance. Experiment with ball position to discover what works for you.

- Routine: Visualize shot; select club; practice swings, as desired; select a close-in target; move to ball; and create silent space.

- Ritual: What is your trigger to commence the swing?

- Drills
  ○ Just let your total body swing the club: hands, arms, and body, naturally; feel the lower body resist the upper body.
  ○ Feel the full shoulder turn and shoulder tilt.
  ○ Feel the transition from the back swing to the forward swing.

- ○ Swing the club and feel the club head; hit a few balls for five minutes for fun.
- ○ *Know distances!*
- ○ Feel the stability of your right leg and lower body as they resist the turn of the shoulders and the upper body. Feel the torque being created and visualize the power being stored. Remember, flat back; wide, stable base; free arm hang; one-piece take-away; stable lower body with hips still; hands in front of toes; left arm straight; and turn, turn, turn till chin hits left shoulder.

The foregoing provides a great deal of material! As mentioned previously, our ability to develop a controlled, consistent game requires patience, persistence, and one step at a time based on where our game is at a given point in time. As we progress in our efforts to become aware, to feel, and to master the technical skills necessary to play a rewarding game, it is important to take time out periodically to assess where we have been, where we are, and where we need to focus development efforts. You may find that collecting key data supports spending practice time on what counts for progress on your game. Some player development data you may find helpful to collect and study are as follows:

- fairways hit
- fairways missed and whether missed left or right
- greens hit in regulation
- greens missed in regulation and whether missed short, long, left, or right
- ups and downs made
- ups and downs missed and why: putt, chip, pitch, etc.
- number of putts
- score
- penalty shots

In conclusion,

- Love putting and the short game.
- Know your distances.
- Accuracy of scoring wedges is a must.
- One thing at a time.
- Play your game.

- Practice what counts for your game.
- Learn to read greens properly.

Let's now put it all together!

CHAPTER 5

Putting It All Together

When we practice enough, we can sit back and enjoy the beauty of the process that flows through us. That is the process of being able to trust our abilities, which lies at the essence of being in the Zone.
—Michael Lardon

The intent of this chapter is not to be an ending but an opportunity for a new beginning, a recharged magnetism, and a self-created fascination for our chosen game. For golfers, the golf course can be a very comfortable studio where creativity can be quietly unbundled. For each round of golf, we select a studio where the wonder of nature, at its purest, emerges. This studio might include a slight breeze, the vivid greens, yellows, and browns of the grasses, a hopping bunny and chirping birds, families of quail hurrying about their business, an array of gorgeous flowers, killdeer "kill-deering" away, the bluest of blue skies with fluffy, cottony clouds, picturesque, majestic mountains with numerous shadows, and an occasional bobcat and slithering snake. The poet within may itch to emerge as you complete the design of your place of work. After all, this is nothing more than being impeccable with your word. How much you love this studio is directly related to the quality and integrity of your inner language in each moment.[8]

As you complete the studio, the zebra-wood easel and an oak painter's stool are given their rightful place. You now begin to stretch a canvas. The concept of studio and canvas returns my thoughts to 2003 and six weeks as a student in

---

[8] Ruiz, 46.

India with Tinlay Gaytso, a Tibetan Buddhist thangka painter. Tinlay's studio was twelve by twelve feet and had two bamboo frame beds with cushions and a small table between the beds that held paints and many paintbrushes.

Thinlay would sit cross-legged on one of the beds, and, as his student, I was on the second bed, sitting cross-legged. Thinlay would painstakingly stretch a single canvas using leather laces to bind it to a rectangular, bamboo-stick frame. He would then treat this canvas with clay until it was impeccable and ready for paint. With the canvas and the top of the bamboo frame suspended from the ceiling with a single string, and the bottom of the frame resting on his knee, Thinlay would begin to paint using a carefully selected brush and a few cups of paint with the colors of the rainbow. If the color was not right, a tad of mixing would make it perfect.

As golfers, our canvas is every hole: the tee, the green, the fairway, the rough, the bunkers, and the hazards, and we have more canvas to unfold with every shot on every hole. Our paint and brushes are our clubs and their dynamics, the ball and its characteristics, and our supple human system that is intent on allowing the programmed subconscious to move a club head through the ball to an intended target. What a wonderful combination of supplies for creating a work of art on every shot in a beautiful studio: a masterpiece that the likes of Ben Hogan or Jack Nicklaus would envy. As Thinlay would constantly remind me, creative expression on the canvas emerges from inner experiences of a chosen image.

It is both our opportunity and our challenge to visualize our golfing canvas carefully and prepare our brushes and paints before we make that first practice swing, smash a drive off the first tee, make a scoring wedge shot, chip it up close, and sink a putt. The game of golf is not easy and requires a massive amount of juggling for creativity to be unleashed on each shot. This sport constantly reminds us that the journey of learning and playing is the destination. As golfers, we paint a canvas with each shot; and regardless of whether we have chosen a path of complexity and chaos or of simplicity and peace of mind, we are each part of a rich history that will continue to evolve for the ages. As George Peper writes in the *Story of Golf*, "No one can say precisely where or when the game of golf was born, but one thing is certain: No other form of recreation has transfixed its practitioners with such engaging appeal."[9] This fascination may exist because of several ingredients:

---

[9] Peper, 13.

- the challenge of learning, practicing, and consistently executing a menu of technical and body-mind skills
- a maturing capacity to have present-moment, silent space for creation of the desired result for every shot
- the opportunity to achieve an optimum level of physical and mental flow to release maximum energy at the point of impact of the clubface through the golf ball to a target
- the enjoyment of the sensual experiences of the mind-body connection and the completed shot
- the magnetism of good relationships
- the goal, desire, and will to improve
- the walk

The smooth integration of inner and outer skills is the ultimate goal for us as we strive to do the best we can on each shot, while at the same time discovering how good we really are at this game. This can be overwhelming at times when one considers the precision golf demands, the insatiable pestering of the inner roommate, the competitive pressures we may choose to encounter, the unique pace of the game, the cultural obsession with body, the club mechanics, and the body-mind demands necessary for a balanced human system. Finding our own synchronized style is really the optimum achievement of the game, and it is a result of total self-awareness as a golfer. This simply means we have to understand and to accept who we are as a person to such an extent that on the golf course we are able to use our unique human system to play an integrated, enjoyable round of golf.

As you choose to move forward with the process of the game, it may prove useful to occasionally take a few moments to reflect on the fruits of your artistry. A nice model for movement from your current reality to vision is to work through three steps:

1. Create a realistic vision for your game.
2. Complete a candid assessment of your current reality. Where have you been with your game? Where is your game today? Where does your game need to go?
3. Develop a list of time-sensitive objectives that are measureable. What needs to be done to create tension to close the gap between where your game is today and your vision?

To facilitate and inspire action planning for your objectives, the balance of this chapter will include: (1) a glimpse of what occurs in the golfer's studio by sharing a student's perspective of the golf shot cycle; (2) a few coaching one liners; (3) a "quick and dirty" skills checklist; and (4) concluding remarks and possible next steps to inspire the creative juices to help you effectively and efficiently move forward with your game. Quite simply, you can unleash the artist within and creatively move from current reality toward your vision.

Golf Shot Cycle

Overview

Prior to making golf shots, most seasoned golfers intuitively choose to put their human system on automatic pilot; they merely go through the motions. With this thought in mind, it may prove fruitful to stop and reflect periodically on two critical parts of the game: (1) that the only purpose of the golf swing is to repetitively move the club through the ball, square to the target, at maximum speed,[10] and (2) that an awareness and understanding of the golf shot cycle has the potential to support performance, enjoyment, and learning at practice and on the course. Even though you may not choose to move consciously through the cycle, my experience has been that it can be helpful to occasionally become conscious of what is transpiring during the process of making shots during a round of golf.

Every golf shot, and its associated cycle, is the opportunity for a peak-performance state—the epitome of a rewarding athletic experience. Juggling the multitude of body-mind and technical skills and targeting for optimal performance is energizing, exciting, and fun. Connected, deep breathing and centering coupled with fluid rhythm and tension-free movement offer the expected performance and opportunities for celebration.

The process of the shot cycle consists of five elements: transition, preparation, action, response, and recovery. Transition is the process of warming up your mental, physical and emotional bodies; preparation unfolds as consistent preround and preshot routines; action is walking to the ball, setting up, and pulling the trigger to create the moment of truth by swinging the club without thought and with unconditional trust in the subconscious to deliver the ball to the desired target. The response is our physical, mental, and emotional behavior following the just-completed shot. And our recovery

---

[10] Jacobs, 13.

includes the activities that help us ready our human system for the next shot. Let's further explore each of the elements.

Transition

Transition could be referred to as the warm-up. It includes the psychological and behavior processes that golfers go through to come to terms with a new situation. Regardless of whether or not the golfer deliberately chooses to experience transition, it happens prior to beginning every round of golf and during the time between every shot during a round of golf. That is a great deal of transition, and it equates to a significant amount of psychological adjustment.

A nice place to begin a discussion of the importance of transition, or change management, is with a basic awareness of the concept as experienced during the golf shot cycle. Transition is the psychological process of moving from an ending to a new beginning; and it implies systematic changes that involve the physical, mental, and emotional bodies of all golfers.

Some of the expected residual effects of an ending might include thoughts and reflections concerning a bad day at work, excitement about a pay raise, loss of a long-term business partnership, attachment to a work associate who was terminated, or needing to learn new policies and procedures. Some of the expected characteristics of a new beginning might include a new sense of purpose for the upcoming round of golf, increased energy and inspiration because of a new back swing, integrating new pieces of the mental and technical elements into the game, or merely being with friends for another nice round of golf.

The characteristics of the neutral zone, or transition, might include a feeling of chaos, a psychological "nowhere," a sense of excitement tension, or relief. For a golfer, one transition time goes from leaving work to starting a preshot routine on the first tee at the start of a round of twilight golf at the local country club. An additional example of a transition is the period from a three-putt green to the next tee just before the golfer begins his or her preshot routine for the next shot.

As mentioned, an abbreviated way of relating to transition is with the term *warm-up*. This process includes the physical, mental, and emotional bodies before a round of golf and before each shot. As Pia Nilsson and Lynn Marriott suggest in *The Game Before the Game*, "A thoughtful transition from the chaos around us to the calm within is necessary to play good golf."[11]

Properly managing transitions can optimize practice and play. You can be very creative with the processes that you use for managing transitions before a round or the next shot. To stimulate your creative juices, consider some of the following:

- Warm up your physical body with a few stretching exercises or a warm-up routine.
- Hit a few balls with two or three clubs.
- Do deep breathing for physical, emotional, and physical relaxation.
- Sit, be silent, and enjoy the solitude of being with nature and friends.
- Make a few chips, pitches, and putts.
- Decide on a swing thought for the round.
- Take a few rehearsal swings to support your tempo, rhythm, and timing.

However you choose to enable your transitions, it is important to recognize that transitions exist and that performance, enjoyment, and learning are enhanced when these periods are creatively facilitated. Quite simply, transition is warming up the human system for peak performance. Coop and Wiren say,

> The state of the body can influence the mood of the mind. In golf, this somatopsychic effect can remove tension in three ways at the physical level, which in turn tends to dissipate tension felt at the mental level:
> - through a preround routine of warm-up drills, which helps the body make the transition from off-course activities to actual play more smoothly
> - through a fixed preshot routine, which keeps the body in a more relaxed state before every shot
> - through a rehearsal-swing routine, which helps the body stay relaxed on short shots and trouble shots that are intrinsically more anxiety producing[12]

---

[11] Marriott and Nilsson, 16.
[12] Coop and Wiren, 156.

Preparation

Preparation is making sure the goal of the shot is crystal clear and that motivation is created to sustain the desired result. This part of the shot cycle has customarily been referred to as the preshot routine. The two tools you have to create for this preparation process are attention and intention. Our attention is the tool of the mental body and is the "what" of our focus. Our intention is the tool of the emotional body and is the "why" of our focus. The quality of each shot experience is determined by how consciously we wield our attention and intention. The only challenge is to be present physically in order to consciously wield these two tools in a way that will serve us.

Attention involves the decision-making process that the analytical left brain goes through prior to making an emotional commitment to the plan and action for each shot. The typical golfer wants this preshot routine to be the same from one shot to the next, and each time you go through the routine you want it to take about the same amount of time. Typically, the routine will include relaxation techniques, target selection, checking the lie of the ball, planning strategies for the wind direction and strength, estimating distance, and making a club selection.

As we confirm the distance and make our club selection, we move behind the ball and possibly stand tall, stretch, pull our shoulders back, lift our chin up, and breathe deeply. We become conscious of the connected, deep breathing and are inspired to feel our center and create a state of relaxed concentration—the personal bubble experienced while standing poised to hit the golf ball. Through awareness, we embrace everything that is creating sensations: sounds, colors, feelings, smells, and physical tensions. Creating a relaxed, tension-free state of mind programs the subconscious with our expectations for the upcoming shot and adds real smell and flavor to the goal we have to accomplish. Using sensual words and mental rehearsal, we bring the shot to life. We visualize the three-dimensional club and body movements of the swing, perhaps coupled with a vivid, felt image of the sensory details of the upcoming event.

The target and its close aiming point are clear as we emotionally energize our inner human system with the "why" the shot is important to us and "what" the benefit of the shot is to the watcher. Rallying the desired motivation requires a flow of inner feelings and personally inspiring words about why the goal is important and what its achievement will do for the golfer. What attributes will the goal provide you? How will you feel about yourself if the goal is realized?

As we complete our preparation, we anticipate the desired state, standing over the golf ball for each shot: we are a human system centered and fully energized for peak performance. This becomes possible in a teepee of self-created space and magic that has become the physical, mental, and emotional aspects of the individual merged into a unified, subconscious activity of hitting a golf ball with perfection in personal silence and solitude.

Before we begin our walk to the ball to create the personal tent for peak performance, we may make a couple practice shots to validate the timing, rhythm, and tempo. Concerning practice swings, Coop and Wiren say, "On anything within 75 yards of the green, on the green itself and for any extra-challenging shot from an unusual lie, a bad position or over an imposing hazard, rehearse the stroke you're going to make at least two or three times as part of your pre-shot routine."[13]

We now have a specific goal, have made clear decisions, and have physically, mentally, and emotionally committed to the plan and strategies chosen. We are energized and motivated and begin our move to the ball.

Action

Action begins with walking to the ball, and it includes set-up, ball positioning, ritual, and centering.[11] As the old Scottish saying goes, "As ye waggle so shall ye swing." We do a body scan to detect and release any tension plus a final look at the target. Then we pull the trigger and trust the subconscious to direct the muscles to perform as they have been trained and programmed. Quite simply, get set up, go through your ritual, get centered with a jig and a little dance, and just let go! Just do it! See it, and either hit it or roll it.

It could be argued that pulling the trigger to make the shot is the most critical of all elements of the shot cycle; however, it may be the simplest and yet the most difficult because it must be done without thinking and with absolute trust in the subconscious to perform to expectations. As we settle in to create the space bubble, we are deliberately breathing. The ritual is automatic and is

---

[13] Coop and Wiren, 72.

[11] Crum, 116. To center, relax any tension you feel through deep breathing and focusing on the present moment and the movement. As you do this, you become less outcome-oriented—that is, less focused on the score, the excuses, or the celebration speeches. Instead, you become process-oriented, focused on the ball, the target, and your center (approximately 1 ½ inch below the belly button). All great athletes go through their ritual, on the tee or before the start of their event. The rituals may be different for each athlete, but they are repeated precisely the same every time for a common reason: to get centered so that their movements happen naturally and appropriately.

the one distinct stimulus that will trigger and coordinate all the elements to create the peak performance state.[15] Accumulating present-moment awareness, we are emotionally charged to "attack" the ball energetically and deliver the intended bone-crushing and square clubface through the ball at impact. We are totally awake, quiet, calm, and relaxed, and we experience silence and solitude as we pull the trigger, listen, and watch.

Hitting good shots comes from commitment: you cannot swing with hesitation; you cannot steer the ball to the flag; you cannot worry about that water hazard as you take the club back. You have to pick the right club, visualize, create an image of the shot you want to hit, and then focus and unleash your energy reservoir as the ball sails and you watch it find its intended target.

When all is said and done, you must believe in your swing and not pull the trigger until you are committed and centered. Thinking is not permitted; however, sense the static and dynamic balance. Feel the center below your belly button, visualize and feel your weight moving back and shifting forward parallel to the target line, and attack the ball. Your swing will get better if you allow your natural athletic ability to shine. Go for it! Stephen Mitchell, in his foreword to the *Tao Te Ching*, writes,

> A good athlete can enter a state of body-awareness in which the right stroke or the right movement happens by itself, effortlessly, without any interference of the conscious will. This is a paradigm for non-action: the purest and most effective form of action. The game plays the game; the poem writes the poem; we can't tell the dancer from the dance.

> Less and less do you need to force things,
> Until finally you arrive at non-action.
> When nothing is done,
> Nothing is left undone.

> Nothing is done because the doer has wholeheartedly vanished into the deed; the fuel has been completely transformed into flame. This is "nothing" is, in fact, everything. It happens when we trust the intelligence of the universe in the same way that an athlete or dancer trusts the superior intelligence of the body.[16]

---

[15] Jordon, 86.
[16] Mitchell, viii.

Response

Yes! Wow! Great shot! The response is the emotional fist and arm pump when Tiger Woods and Rory McIlroy sink that critical putt on the eighteenth green to win $1.5 million. This is an open acknowledgment of the thrill and excitement of watching the beauty of a ball's trajectory, hearing the sound of the club and ball at impact, or seeing the ball hit the green, bounce, and come to rest near the pin. This is celebrating the bunker shot that leaves a four-foot putt; and this is jumping into the air and letting the world know you just made that first hole-in-one.

Needless to say, we need to manage our negative emotions, too. An errant golf shot is a fine opportunity to acknowledge our reflections in the world and learn from them. These errant shots can help us surface and integrate subconscious behaviors and certainly can support learning to dampen the detrimental impact that the dreaded demon of tension can have on our golf game. These challenges can also support our efforts to mentally track, know, and learn the nine ball flight effects and their respective body and club mechanics causes. This can provide great information to help you facilitate swing changes during that next practice session. Concerning response to good shots, Coop and Wiren say,

> Psychologist Peter Cranford draws the analogy that a good round of golf is a string of pearls. Each shot is a precious pearl that takes your full attention to create. You can only create one at a time, so don't concern yourself with those you have already made or those you have yet to make. Focusing on adding one pearl, individually, leads to the creation of a fine finished product.[17]

Recovery

Recovery is relaxing—enjoying nature, relationships, and the opportunity to learn; being grateful for the quality of the experiences offered by golf; relieving tension; and time for insight and freedom. Smell the roses, enjoy the day, take a deep breath, smile, and be at peace. As the period of recovery nears its end, it includes transitioning your body-mind for the next encounter with the new canvas, your artist's tools, a golf ball, and the associated challenges of the next shot.

---

[17] Coop and Wiren, 114.

Recovery is nothing more than the interlude before starting preparation for a next shot, which will require optimum relaxation, attention, intention, and trust. Recovery restores health to the human system and may include deep breathing, deliberate relaxation, enjoyment, relating, learning, gratitude, and preliminary thoughts about the next shot. *I am centered, calm, silent, present, and at peace. My choice is to experience this moment.*

In conclusion, connected, deep breathing, a good tempo and timing, and tension-free movement are the means to a journey of wonderful, peak experiences. The shot cycle is a metaphor for our life cycle of life: its events, activities, and moments. We have the opportunity to recycle a quality of life that consciously, or subconsciously, is symptomatic of needing improvement; or we can embrace the dance of life and improve the quality of our experiences. The choice rests with each of us: as every shot has a purpose, every moment of life has a purpose that we can choose to embrace and energize. Whether our choice is to live in the past or the future, we are living in time, and we spend our life seeking the meaning of life. In the present moment, we enjoy a life saturated with meaning.[18]

The quality of our golf swing and the quality of our life experiences depend on uncovering and nourishing causes that make a lasting difference. Our mutual challenge is to experience interconnectedness and joy with our self and with those around us. Culturally, our lives become so effect-driven that seldom do we take the time to gather insight that uncovers causes that can evolve lasting changes in the quality of our experiences in life and in golf.

Dealing with effects is temporary, cyclic, and frustrating. Some tools that you may find helpful in uncovering "shot cycle" causes of stress and the related mental, physical, and emotional tensions are as follows:

- Body-mind mastery is an essential ingredient for the experiences of authentic joy, abundance, and health. A nice process guide to consider is *The Presence Process: A Healing Journey into Present Moment Awareness* by Michael Brown.
- Find a meditation instructor and learn to meditate. Meditation can be an asset on the golf course and in life. Connected breathing and centering can enable development of our will to act in spite of what is happening outside of us. Being the "watcher" and preparing and trusting the inner presence to perform is warming, enjoyable, and healthy.

---

[18] Brown, 144.

- Work with your golf shot cycle. It can be as rewarding and fun as you choose to make it; and it can be a wonderful self-awareness vehicle. Do the best you can on every shot, and uncover just how good you can be.
- Be open to discovery, new ideas, and learning; fully participate in golf and life.
- Become aware of and use your emotional triggers to learn peak performance skills: centering, deep breathing, rhythm, and tension-free, high quality of movement.[19]
- Practice your art of static balance and dynamic centering, "the highest degree of mobility with a center which remains immovable."[20] As Tom Crum says, "Ben Hogan didn't write that? He certainly played with an immovable center. Arms, shoulders, hips, everything else flowed around his center with power and grace."[21]

Have fun, enjoy, perform, learn, and master the golf shot cycle. Just be centered, mindful, and aware. Swing the golf club to flow energy of the club head square to the target line and through the ball at maximum speed.

Coaching One-Liners

- Review your vision, current reality, objectives, and action plans. Based on where your game is today, fine tune your objectives and action plans.
- Arrange to take a playing lesson with a good coach:
    - ✓ Prior to the scheduled date of play, complete a "shot cycle game plan" with your coach by discussing and agreeing on specific roles, focuses, and objectives for the scheduled date of the playing lesson.
    - ✓ Schedule a date of play on the course with the shot cycle game plan.
- Create a mind and body warm-up process to use before you play.
- Develop a consistent preshot routine for each type of shot.
- Become a body-mind master through a contemplative practice that works for you.
  -Learn to meditate-in-action between shots.
  -Learn to trust the subconscious to perform.

---

[19] Jordon, 35–50.
[20] Crum, 114.
[21] Ibid., 114.

-Learn and practice deliberately creating a clear and quiet, tension-free, peace of mind prior to pulling the trigger for each shot.

- Master the synchronization of your inner and outer games.
- Play your game and practice what counts for your game.
- Love putting and the short game.
- Be a good student of the game.
- Track playing data that efficiently and effectively target areas for improvement of your game.
- Know why you play the game, and play the game to satisfy that purpose.
- Practice and learn to be your own best coach and caddie.
- Model the way as a person, in relationships, and when enabling others.
- Accept 100 percent responsibility: life happens because of me and not to me.

"Quick and Dirty" Skills Checklist

Learning and Practice

- ✓ Practice putting, chipping, pitching, and sand shots (these are 60 percent of your shots).
- ✓ Practice what counts for your game.
- ✓ Learn awareness, which is an excellent way to learn and practice.

Body-Mind

- ✓ Master creating your personal teepee for every shot.[22]
- ✓ Relaxed warm-up time and process.
- ✓ Follow an effective exercise program: strength, endurance, and power; cardiovascular, weight training, and stretching.
- ✓ Practice concentration, meditation, and contemplation processes that work for you.
- ✓ Focus on nutrition, posture, relaxation, tension reduction, and rest.

---

[22] Gallwey, "Relaxed Concentration: The Master Skill," 169–85; Shoemaker, "Concentration," 50–60, 195–96. The human mind has an inner roommate that pesters and a "watcher" that is the sentinel. In a state of relaxed concentration the inner roommate is absent, and the watcher is present and abiding. As used in this book, this is the natural state of the subconscious. As golfers, it is important to grasp that concentration of thought cannot occur unless the watcher has learned and practiced guiding the flow of thought, taming the monkey mind, and quieting the patterns of interference.

- ✓ Use preventive health care.
- ✓ Trust the subconscious to perform.
- ✓ Acknowledge your reflections in the world.
- ✓ Be positive when speaking to yourself: we get back what we put out.

Technical

- ✓ Learn to feel static and dynamic balance.
- ✓ Develop an impeccable set-up: 80 to 85 percent of a good, consistent swing.
- ✓ Visualize the plane and swing center of an effective swing: now at 90 percent of a consistent swing.
- ✓ Maintain a stable right side during the backswing.
- ✓ Remember the one-piece take-away: your club, hands, and arms move as a single unit: now at 95 percent of a good swing.
- ✓ Make a good shoulder turn and shoulder tilt.
- ✓ Finish the backswing, and do not rush the forward swing; energy will accumulate prior to impact.
- ✓ Stay down with the ball, and hit through the ball to the target.
- ✓ Learn to love the short game.
- ✓ Make every putt: start the ball on your chosen *line* at the desired *speed* and with a *stroke* that feels good.
- ✓ Know your distances.
- ✓ Accuracy of scoring wedges is a must.
- ✓ Have equipment that fits and feels good.

Concluding Remarks and Possible Next Steps

The golf industry needs new, visionary leaders who can sculpt a future and intentionally influence and coach others to move from current reality toward a future that serves individuals, families, communities, and an evolving human consciousness.

Contemplative golf students can offer unique "new age" skills to this fascinating sport; and golf coaches and instructors need to place students first and the game of golf second. Pia Nilsson and Lynn Marriott are two instructors who are on the leading edge of "a revolution going on in the way golf is being taught … Many teachers are recognizing that golf is about much more than arm angles and swing slots ... Lynn and Pia will help you learn how to live your life, not watch it."[23]

As we look around the globe, the chaos can be overwhelming: terrorism, wars, violence, shootings, environmental degradation, global warming, and the list can go on and on. A deep look can lead us to conclude that the root cause of these effects is the level of our human consciousness. Of necessity, our consciousness must evolve to a new level. As Bruce Lipton and Steve Bhaerman write in *Spontaneous Evolution*,

> Through the evolution of humanity, we will come to see Earth not as a physical planet but as a living cell. What happens when a cell fulfills its evolution? It assembles into colonies with other evolved cells to share awareness ... Consequently, the real challenge for the individual is to practice evolution, to learn the lessons of the old stories so we no longer need to repeat them, and to remind ourselves that the critical mass of humanity involved with this evolution will change the world from the inside out. We are living in a positive future, practicing Heaven, and designing a bridge across which the whole of humanity will walk.[21]

This new earth evolves as each individual makes one step at a time. Awareness of our experiences is our best teacher. Life dances to our dance. In the context of Army Black Knights football, General of the Army Douglas MacArthur wrote, "Upon the fields of friendly strife are sown the seeds that upon other fields, on other days, will bear the fruits of victory." The same can be said of the wonderful sport of golf. The Dalai Lama says,

> Within the scale of the life of the cosmos, a human life is no more than a tiny blip. Each one of us is a visitor to this planet, a guest, who has only a finite time to stay. What greater folly could there be than to spend this short time lonely, unhappy, and in conflict with our fellow visitors? Far better, surely, to use our short time in pursuing a meaningful life, enriched by a sense of connection with and service toward others.[25]

---

[23] Nilsson and Marriott, 13.
[21] Bhaerman and Lipton, 358–59.
[25] Dali Lama, 188.

As a parting note, whether on the course or off the course, Don Miguel Ruiz offers in *The Four Agreements* a powerful code of conduct that can rapidly transform our lives to a new experience of freedom, true happiness, and love:

- Be impeccable with your word.
- Don't take anything personally.
- Don't make assumptions.
- Always do your best.[26]

Larry Root, my good friend and the head PGA golf professional at Stoney Creek Golf Course, Arvada, Colorado, would always remark, as my wife, Cindy, and I left the clubhouse for the first tee, "Hit 'em high, hit 'em straight, and make those three-foot putts." As playing and competing members in this unique and legendary culture of golfers, our mutual goal is to be in the moment and to reveal the artist within through golf and life. To play our best game—in golf and life—requires programming of the subconscious and learning to trust our supple, golfer's system to perform. Through our innate, inspired energies, we can evolve a personal palette of skills and talents and forge action plans that will reveal the creative golfers we are. Be patient, learn, practice, practice, practice, and practice some more. Embrace body-mind mastery and the plethora of technical skills. Be happy and enjoy playing golf and living life as you intend it to be.

---

[26] Ruiz, 25–91.

BIBLIOGRAPHY

Armour, T. *How to Play Your Best Golf All the Time*. New York: Simon & Schuster, 1953.

Bhaerman, S., and B. Lipton. *Spontaneous Evolution: Our Positive Future (and a way to get there from here)*. New York: Hay, 2009.

Bhodan, D. A. *The Lazy Man's Way to Enlightenment: What You're Looking For Is What Is Looking*. New York: Right Now, 2012.

Brown, M. *The Presence Process: A Healing Journey Into Present Moment Awareness*. New York: Beaufort, 2005.

Coop, R., and G. Wiren. *The New Golf Mind*. New York: Simon & Schuster, 1978.

Crittenden, J. "The future of golf according to Dana Garmany," *Golf Inc.*, Spring 2010, 28–31.

Crum, T. F. *Journey to Center: Lessons in Unifying Body, Mind, and Spirit*. New York: Fireside, 1977.

DeVito, C. *Golf: The Players, The Tournaments, The Records*. Kennebunkport, ME: Cider Mill Press, 2008.

Gimian, J. *Be the Change: How Meditation Can Transform You and the World*. New York: Sterling, 2009.

Gallwey, W. T. *The Inner Game of Golf*. rev. ed. New York: Random House, 1998.

Goldstein, J. *Insight Meditation: The Practice of Freedom*. Boston: Shambhala, 1994.

Golf Academy of America Teaching Manual. 2nd ed. Chandler, AZ, www. golfacademy.edu, 2009.

His Holiness the Dalai Lama. *Beyond Religion: Ethics for a Whole World.* Boston: Houghton Mifflin Harcourt, 2010.

Jacobs, J. *Practical Golf.* Guilford, Connecticut: Lyons, 1972.

Lardon, M., and D. Leadbetter. *Finding Your Zone: Ten Core Lessons for Achieving Peak Performance in Life and Sport.* New York: Penguin, 2008.

Lipton, B. H. *The Biology of Belief.* New York: Hay, 2005.

Love, D., Jr., and B. Toski. *How to Feel a Real Golf Swing: Mind-Body Techniques from Two of Golf's Greatest Teachers.* New York: Three Rivers, 1997.

Marriott, L., and P. Nilsson. *Play Your Best Golf Now.* New York: Gotham, 2010.

_____. *The Game Before the Game.* New York: Gotham, 2007.

Millman, D. *Body Mind Mastery: Creating Success in Sport and Life.* Novato, CA: New World Library, 1999.

Mitchell, S. *Tao Te Ching.* New York: Harper, 1988.

Murphy, M. *Golf in the Kingdom.* New York: Penguin, 1972.

Parent, J. *Zen Golf: Mastering the Mental Game.* New York: Doubleday, 2002.

Pelz, D. *Dave Pelz's Putting Bible: The Complete Guide to Mastering the Green.* New York: Doubleday, 2000.

_____. *Dave Pelz's Short Game Bible: Master the Finesse Swing and Lower Your Score.* New York: Aurum, 1999.

Peper, G. *The Story of Golf.* New York: TV Books, 1995.

Reid, C. *Get Yourself in Golf Shape: Year-Round Drills to Build a Strong, Flexible Swing.* New York: Rodale, 2005.

Rotella, B. *The Golfer's Mind: Play to Play Great.* New York: Free Press, 2004.

————. *The Unstoppable Golfer: Trusting Your Mind & Your Short Game to Achieve Greatness.* New York: Free Press, 2012.

Ruiz, D. *The Four Agreements: A Toltec Wisdom Book.* San Rafael, CA: Amber Allen, 1997.

Sakyong Mipham. *Turning the Mind Into an Ally.* New York: Riverhead, 2003.

Schaef, A. W., and D. Fassel. *The Addictive Organization: Why We Overwork, Cover Up the Pieces, Please the Boss and Perpetuate.* San Francisco: Harper & Row, 1988.

Shapiro, E., and D. Shapiro. *Be the Change: How Meditation Can Transform You and the World.* New York: Sterling Ethos, 2011.

Shoemaker, F. *Extraordinary Golf: The Art of the Possible.* New York: Pedigree, 1996.

Tolle, E. *A New Earth: Awakening to Your Life's Purpose.* New York: Plume, 2005.

————. *The Power of Now: A Guide to Spiritual Enlightenment.* Novato: CA: New World, 1999.

Toski, B. *The Touch System for Better Golf.* Norwalk, CT: Golf Digest, 1977.

Toski, B., and Davis Love Jr. *How to Feel a Real Golf Swing: Mind-Body Techniques from Two of Golf's Greatest Teachers.* New York: Three Rivers, 1997.

ABOUT THE AUTHOR

Dr. John Edwin DeVore

- 2013, advanced teaching, The Golf Academy of America.
- 2011, graduate, The Golf Academy of America.
- Academic credentials: PhD in human communication and MBA, University of Denver; MA in religious studies, Naropa University; BS in military art and engineering, United States Military Academy, West Point, New York; and associate of business in golf management, The Golf Academy of America.
- Military service: United States Army, eight years, including two years of combat during the Vietnam War; Airborne, Ranger, well decorated and honorable discharge as major.
- Corporate leadership and management executive and consultant, twenty-seven years.
- Published author: *Sitting in the Flames: Uncovering Fearlessness to Help Others*, 2014; and *Golfer's Palette: Preparing for Peak Performance*, 2014.
- President and owner, Golf-Life Mastery, a golf coaching business.
- Golf: sixty-seven years.
  -First set of clubs was a Wilson putter, a five iron, and a brassy. Playing partners were Mom and Dad. We played at Orchard Hills Country Club, Bryan, Ohio. Our coach was Shorty Stockman. Dad's golf ball of choice was the Wilson K-28.
  -Second set of clubs, used for fifty years, was a matched set of Wilson, Sam Snead, woods and irons. This set of clubs was given by Mom to Dad on their twenty-fifth wedding anniversary. These clubs were passed along when they became too heavy for Dad. When Mom passed away in 1955, Dad played with Mom's clubs: a matched set of Wilson, Babe Didrikson Zaharius, woods and irons.
- Contact Information:
  www.johnedwindevore.com
  E-mail: JohnDeVore@aol.com

CPSIA information can be obtained at www.ICGtesting.com
Printed in the USA
LVOW11s2310230215

428028LV00005B/52/P